ADVANCED DRIVING

The official RoSPA book of advanced motoring

GORDON COLE

First published 1986
First reprint 1988
Second reprint 1990
Second Edition 1993

ISBN 0 7110 2131 7

Published by Ian Allan Ltd, Shepperton, Surrey; and printed by Ian Allan Printing Ltd at their works at Coombelands in Runnymede, England.

Acknowledgements

I would like to thank the following Police forces for their co-operation; without it, some of the photographs could not have been taken:

Hertfordshire Constabulary
Bedfordshire Police
Thames Valley Police
Metropolitan Police

References and extracts are from:

Department of Transport Highways Economics Note 1 (November 1991): Road Accident Costs

Roadcraft

(Material from both publications is reproduced by permission of the Controller of Her Majesty's Stationary Office)

Psychology: Human Factors in Driver Training and Education, Dr L. E. Schlesinger

The History of the Metropolitan Police Motor Driving School, Hendon, Bill Fleming

Accident statistics supplied by RoSPA.

Vehicles supplied by Vauxhall Motors, Luton.

All Photography was by the author, using Leica cameras and lenses.

Gordon Cole,
Stevenage,
April 1993

About the author:
Gordon Cole is a Driving Training Consultant, and can provide theoretical and practical assistance for Advanced, Defensive and Approved Driving Instructor Training (ADI). He can be contacted by telephone on either (0438) 815203 or (0850) 789294 for further information on the above.

Contents

Foreword

The RoSPA Advanced Drivers Association with its untiring workforce of dedicated volunteers is pleased to be identified in working with the advanced driving principles and advice contained in this book. Every driver of whatever age or experience will find something in the contents to provoke thought, recall personal experience and most importantly promote the continuous process of advancement in driving knowledge and application. On a personal note I must commend Gordon Cole for his attention to detail and aim at perfection.

R. L. Smalley
Chief Examiner
RoSPA Advanced Drivers Association

Introduction

At the end of 1991 there were over 34 million people holding UK driving licences. They represent most nationalities and all walks of life. Their attitude to life and to other peoples' safety, can vary considerably. They all have the privilege of having a licence to drive a motor vehicle; how they drive is another matter, as accident reports and statistics prove. Advanced Driving was formulated for the police many years ago, by the late Earl of Cottenham, who was a racing driver of some note. His aim was to reduce the number and severity of road accidents in which police drivers were involved, which even at that time, 1937, was far too high, whether or not engaged on emergency calls. In an endeavour to achieve this, he introduced a technique of advanced driving at the Hendon Police Driving School which became known as 'The System of Car Control'. Briefly, his System was, that by implementing a simple 'drill' or sequence of events, a driver would ensure that his vehicle was always in the right place on the road at the right time, travelling at the right speed and in the correct gear. Thus, it was reasoned, a driver should be in complete control of the car and any situation with which he might be faced. This is the basis on which advanced driving was built. Together with the right thinking and attitudes, you too can learn the perception and cognitive skills that are required to assist you to become a better driver.

There is a lot to be gained from advanced driving, which will be learned as the content within these pages are studied. This book, *Advanced Driving*, has been described as roadcraft in pictures, and that is the intention.

1 Advanced Driving

The prevention of road accidents has been a matter for concern for numerous government and safety organisations. To assist the Department of Transport and other organisations to promote road safety, the private sector in commerce and industry has donated large sums of money, and/or publicity material to assist the department and others to achieve their objective. To give some idea as to the volume of people who use our overcrowded roads, the following data defines the drivers who hold a full (substantive) licence, and those who hold a provisional driving licence. The figures supplied by the DVLA (Driver and Vehicle Licensing Agency) do not include drivers who visit the UK each year, or have occupational ties of a definite duration of less than 185 days.

By the end of 1991, over 17,905,00 Full driving licences were issued to men, and 12,005,000 Full driving licences to women. The number of people who held a provisional driving licence was 1,830,000 men and 2,780,000 women. There were also 24,750,000 licenced vehicles in the United Kingdom and 9,720,000 unlicenced vehicles which were not being used for one reason or another.

In 1951 road accident statistics were first made available in their present, albeit less detailed, format. At that time there was a vehicle population of 4.7 million and there were 178,000 personal injury road accidents. In 1990 the vehicle population stood at 24.7 million and there were 258,441 recorded road accidents in which 5,217 men, women and children died.

The principal purpose of collecting and publishing statistics of road accidents is to provide background information on such matters as the roads, places, times of day, weather conditions, etc where road accidents happen. These statistics are used to stimulate informed debate on matters of road safety, and to provide both a local and national perspective for particular road safety problems or particular suggested remedies. Most of the analyses within road accident statistics are based on reports sent to the Department of Transport by police forces, using the accident report form known as STATS 19. The current system of collecting road accident statistics was set up in 1968. Each year some 259,000 STATS 19 road accident report forms are completed by officers of the 51 police forces in Great Britain about road accidents on the public highway which included human injury or death.

Human error is the cause of 90% of all road accidents. Thus it can be said that once the Department of Transport 'L' test has been passed, the majority of drivers/riders who have done so, forget or ignore the advice given in the illustrated *Highway Code*, thereby allowing their standard of driving to deteriorate in many ways. They drift into bad habits which they often see in other drivers and which they think are better, easier or just convenient. Therefore the dangerous mistakes they commit are to some the beginning of their end, or that of another road user or pedestrian, because of their ignorant, selfish or arrogant attitude.

Remember that the basics of motoring skills, which you were taught, should be the foundation on which you should build your driving career.

Accident reports have proved time and time again — accidents don't just happen they are caused. It is common knowledge any fool can driver or ride a motor vehicle — and a lot of them do.

Most of us have seen a road accident at one time or another; we know how it happened but not always why. It only takes one thoughtless driver, cyclist or pedestrian to cause a lot of pain, suffering and damage to property.

The motor car has been designed to start, stop, go forwards, backwards, turn left and right. This must be done in complete safety, creating no inconvenience or danger to any other road user or pedestrian while travelling in whatever direction. However, accident statistics over many years inform us that around 5,000 people are killed on roads in the Uk each year. What a waste of life and money this figure represents.

The enthusiasm for Advanced and Defensive Driving is encouraging, not only because of the personal gain in financial benefits and pleasure which can be derived from having the ability to drive to the high standard required to pass the Advanced Driving Test, but because of the satisfaction that a person can prove, by examination, that he or she is a safer and more competent driver than their next door neighbour or colleague at work.

There are three factors which can cause a road accident: human error; mechanical failure; and the environment. In some accidents two factors are the cause, but very rarely do all three interact. Statistics have proved that in nine out of 10 accidents, the causation factor can be traced to human error. Of course, road accidents can happen in all types of weather, on all types of road, at all times of the day and night.

Driving includes making sure the vehicles, passengers, and any load is safe, and complies with the law before starting the engine, moving off, accelerating at the right time and place. Steering the vehicle over different types of roads and surfaces, round corners and bends, in and out of different types of premises, overtake moving and passing stationary vehicles with safety is essential. Drive at the appropriate speed for the conditions, using the correct gear, rear view mirrors and direction indicator signals, and stop the vehicle safely. All this must be done in complete safety, with no inconvenience to others and with minimum wear to the vehicle, regardless where the vehicle is driven.

It is therefore of the utmost importance that a driver has a thorough understanding of the workings of an engine and transmission system. This knowledge, combined with intelligent use of the accelerator, clutch, gears and brakes, will enable the driver to change gear with smoothness and in complete safety, with minimum wear to the vehicle. This consideration for the vehicle is the hallmark of an expert professional driver, who will gain maximum efficiency from the engine, and in return will achieve economical motoring which is part of the ultimate aim of Advanced Driving.

A driver with a good understanding of the controls of his/her vehicle, who drives smoothly and unobtrusively, who is alert but looks relaxed, who knows the capabilities and handling characteristics of the vehicle being driven, who combines this knowledge with good powers of concentration, observation, anticipation and patience, will recognise potential danger well in advance and act on what is seen in a controlled and systematic manner; this is a hallmark of the expert, who omits no detail and leaves nothing to chance.

The driver will always be in the correct place on the road, travelling at the correct speed with the correct gear engaged. This desirable state is achieved by concentrating all the time, planning ahead and driving systematically, which is essential to ensure that the driver does not put him/herself, passenger(s) or any other road user or pedestrian in a potentially dangerous situation, at any time or place.

2 The Requirements of a Driver

As already noted, human error is the cause of the majority of road accidents. This can be attributed to numerous factors. For example, did the drivers involved in the accidents have poor perceptual, cognitive skills or psychomotor function, or did some of the drivers have something on their mind, other than driving at the time, whereby lack of concentration could have been a contributory factor to the cause of the accident.

The thought(s) and attitude of a driver start when a person decides to drive a motor vehicle on the public highway. That is the moment their driving career starts. How some novice drivers approach their task to acquire the necessary knowledge and skills required to pass the 'L' Driving Test is another matter. If a sloppy, 'could not care less' attitude to the textbook way to which a vehicle should be driven is adopted by a novice driver, and the advice given in the *Highway Code* is classed as irrelevant, then there is little hope of installing the responsible attitude required to drive a motor vehicle into a character with a mindless opinion of driving, regardless of their own or other peoples' safety.

Perceptual Motor Skills

A driver has a great deal to think about and see, as conditions are continually changing, more so when travelling at speed. As speed is increased the driver should automatically focus his/her eyes and attention further ahead. Perception is observation, seeing and assessing the road ahead. This assists a driver in judgment and decision making, which will enable a safe driving plan to be made.

Guidance: Search, Identification and Prediction

The **guidance task**, or perceptual task as it is sometimes called, can be broken down into three subtasks: search, identification and prediction. The procedures of performing these subtasks tell the driver where and when to look, what to look for and what to make of it. The subtasks answer the questions: is anything going on that could influence my driving? Search consists of observational behaviours used by the driver to note the presence or absence of critical characteristics of the driving environment. Identification requires the classification of these observations according to their information content. Prediction involves the future conditions of the environment and the vehicular system from the present available information. Efficient and accurate performance of these guidance procedures provides the driver with the ability to quickly characterise the present driving situation, predict the accident potential of developing situations and plan the steps that will carry him/her along the route safely and efficiently.

Cognitive Skills

Cognitive skill is the ability to learn, an ability which exists in everyone. To what extent the information is absorbed and remembered

Below:

By looking across the bend a pedestrian can be seen. The mirror should be used and a reduction of speed considered, even though the road beyond the pedestrian seems to be clear. This must not be taken for granted, as the situation can change.

All photographs by the author

can, however, vary considerably between one person and another. This applies particularly to learning the numerous facets apertaining to driving a motor vehicle, which have to be known and implemented, to be able to drive a motor vehicle in complete safety. To gain further knowledge in the art of driving a motor vehicle, some drivers attend Advance Driving, Defensive or Driver Improvement courses. Learning is a gradual process. Experience cannot be bought, it has to be learned with assistance from professional instruction.

Control: Decision-making and Execution

Accurate prediction enables the driver to formulate alternative actions, select the most satisfactory and execute the required manoeuvre. The **control task**, then, can be broken down into two subtasks: decision-making and execution. Decision-making procedures are concerned with the question of what to do and execution obviously with the driver's responses to the vehicle. In approaching a traffic sign, for example, the driver must decide whether to stop, where to stop and how hard and when the brake pedal should be used. Then he/she must carry out the appropriate control actions. Decision-making involves the cognitive selection of response alternatives based on the information gained from performance of the information-processing subtasks. Execution involves the driver's input to the vehicle (using the controls) and feedback (response) from the vehicle to the driver, a psychomotor cybernetic task that operates within the larger servo melanism outlined in Figure 1.

Psychomotor Function

The psychomotor function of a driver is the ability to recognise and understand a given situation, and be able to implement a correct course of action. For example, the eyes observe potential danger and inform the brain, which instructs the appropriate limb(s) to use the relative control(s) of the vehicle, thereby taking the necessary action.

A driver may have poor powers of concentration, observation, anticipation and patience and may therefore be inclined to be aggresive. He or she may be unable to use the appropriate controls of the vehicle with delicacy and precision as the situation demands. Perhaps because of inadequate knowledge of the workings and mechanics of the vehicle he or she is driving, the driver will have little or no respect for the vehicle — and in return will have poor co-ordination between himself and his vehicle. This can be dangerous at any given time and place. The driver and vehicle must be in unison at all times. It is essential to be in control of a vehicle and in complete control of yourself both physically and mentally, in order to be able to respond to any situation which could arise.

There are two classes of behaviour required of the driver:

(1) guidance: the cybrenetic task of obtaining and processing information from the environment;

(2) control: the task of translating guidance data into decisions and psychomotor control of the vehicle.

These guidance and control functions enable the driver-vehicle unit to move forward at a rate and direction partly determined by the environment, and to maintain separation from other vehicles and objects.

Objective of Driver Training, Training Methods, Evaluation Techniques

It has been reported that accident-free drivers could be distinguished from accident-producing drivers by their methods of observing the driving scene. The accident-free drivers, had developed systematic observational routines, while the accident prone drivers gave more time to vehicular control and non-driving stimuli such as scenery, events inside the vehicle and personal thoughts.

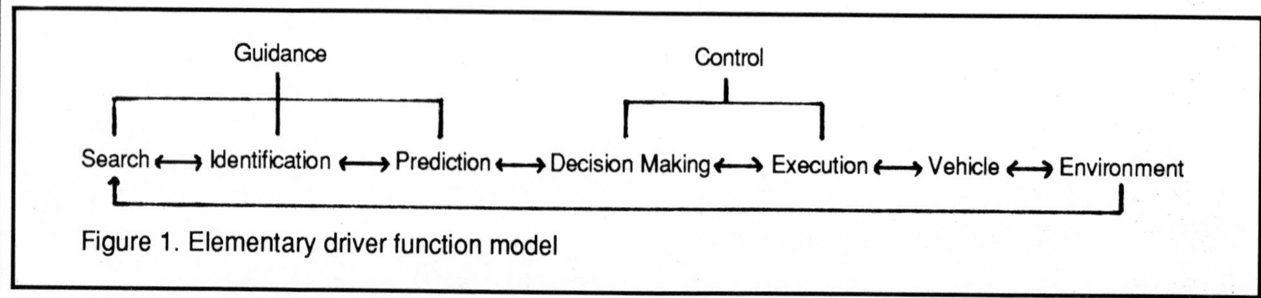

Figure 1. Elementary driver function model

Left:
Vehicles can be seen waiting to emerge on to a roundabout. An accurate prediction must be formulated before the decision can be made to emerge on to the roundabout; otherwise an accident could occur.

Search may be defined as the observational procedures used to note the presence or absence of critical objects or differences in the driving scene. The search subtasks may be further subdivided into at least three compartments:

(a) focus of attention; (b) search rate; (c) search pattern.

'Focus of attention' refers to where and what the driver looks at as he/she confront an ever-changing environment. This focus may need to change with speed, visibility, road topography, traffic volume and density. 'Search rate' is concerned with how frequently the driver searches his environment.

The problem here is one of time sampling; what portion of his time should the driver spend in looking at the various elements of his environment such as: the current location of his vehicle?; the road ahead, behind, and to either side?; the instruments in the vehicle? The third component, 'Search pattern', is concerned with how efficiently the driver samples his environment. For example, in overtaking a vehicle should the driver use a consistent search procedure pattern, such as looking well ahead for oncoming traffic, and to the rear to be certain that if the need should arise there is room to return to the pre-overtaking position in the event of an emergency? Scanning and search routine is, therefore, a requirement for efficient driving.

Above:
By looking well ahead significant clues to potential danger can be seen: the undulating road has dead ground in numerous places: sheep can be seen wandering in the road. Therefore the mirror should be used and speed reduced. The use of the horn can be considered, but if used, it must not be taken for granted that the sheep will move off the road.

Training in Identification

Recognition of critical cues in driving requires a capacity to detect and classify environmental changes that may require compensatory action. The role of training in identification is to provide the trainee with a set of instructions telling him 'what to look for' and provide practice in these procedures. Although a great deal of theoretical information may be gained from the author's list of illustrated driver manuals and training programmes about driving/riding cues that signify danger, in which systematic routines to identify the significant clues in the environment and the vehicle have been evaluated. It is, however, by practice in sharpening recognition skills that drivers may increase their proficiency in identifying clues to potentially dangerous situations.

Prediction

Prediction refers to the translation of varied information into possible future outcomes on the basis of 'rules' stored in the memory. These rules include:

(a) explicit rules of the road;
(b) 'rules' having to do with human behaviour in general;
(c) 'rules' of vehicular dynamics derived from driving experience.

These rules form the basis of most predictions the driver must make concerning the control of the vehicle being driven and his interaction with other drivers and other traffic.

Training in the perceptual functions — observation, identification and interpretation — may benefit by the technique of 'commentary driving' (thinking aloud). This method of training in the perceptual functions has been used by the police motor driving schools in the United Kingdom for many years. The driver comments on the hazards perceived, the possible hazards impending and his/her plans to avoid them. Commentary driving increases the sensitivity of drivers to the requirement for observational routines, clue identification and interpretation of the problems presented by the driving task. Drivers become aware of distraction, the clue they are missing and problems they had not thought of solving. The role of self-instruction, verbal plans and strategies in the acquisition of motor skills can be assisted with the use of a tape recorder, whereby the driver's thoughts can be replayed and analysed.

Training in Execution

A number of research studies comparing different methods of training drivers in using the controls of the vehicle have been reported. These studies typically are concerned with comparing range, on-the-road and simulator training. Unfortunately, none of the studies has dealt with the content of the training, the main focus has been on method. Training in speed and directional control and road positioning is primarily teaching a motor skill. Learning a motor skill requires the stimulation provided by kinesthetic feedback from the muscles — 'getting the feel of the car'. Practice in a vehicle on a variety of roads is essential for learning this skill.

About two million 'L' driving tests are conducted each year in the United Kingdom. Statistics compiled from the result of the tests show that about 53% of candidates fail. This figure proves that some driving test candidates are not up to the basic standard of competence to drive. Some of the candidates did not have the perceptual, cognitive skills or the necessary knowledge to be able to make the correct decision(s) (psychomotor function), due to inadequate training. Some test candidates knew this, but still took the test.

There are some who have passed the test by luck and not by skill, because they did not encounter a situation during their test with which they were not competent to cope, should it have arisen.

Knowing this, the new so-called 'qualified' driver still takes to the road under the misconception that he/she knows all about driving. If novice drivers were keen to learn to drive to an efficient standard, instead of trying to obtain a driving licence as cheaply and as quickly as possible, then a major contribution to road safety would be made.

Another factor in the road safety equation is if the people who use our roads each day allowed sufficient time for their journey, took more interest in their driving and concentrated on the road ahead and the prevailing conditions, instead of irrelevant matters and using their vehicle as the means of travelling from point 'A' to point 'B' as quickly as possible. Accepting sensible journey times and greater concentration by all drivers would bring a significant contribution to making our overcrowded roads safer to use.

If proof were ever needed that good driving pays a handsome dividend in safety on the road, then a classic example would be that of police officers who have attended and passed the numerous driving courses at Police Motor Driving Schools throughout the United Kingdom. Having reached the highest possible standard required of that establishment for the officer to be authorised to drive a particular class of vehicle, or vehicles, in police forces throughout Great Britain. Another significant point is that police drivers keep themselves fit to drive, which assists them to be alert at all times.

It has been confirmed that members of The Institute of Advanced Motorists and RoSPA Advanced Drivers' Association have made their contribution to road safety, by proving their driving is well above the average standard. And, indeed, the members of the Guild of Experienced Motorists have made their contribution to road safety by driving with care, courtesy and concentration.

The Vehicle

Each year vehicle manufacturers and their component suppliers make a major contribution to road safety by spending millions of pounds on research and development. With the results of the knowledge gained, vehicles and components are being produced with many primary and secondary safety features built into them. Primary safety areas are steering, brakes (eg ABS — Anti-lock Braking System), chassis and construction, all of which are contributory factors in avoiding accidents.

The secondary safety features are a cabin safety cell for passenger compartment and crumple zones front and rear, which will protect the driver and passengers from injury in the event of an accident.

Needless to say, primary features which improve the road-holding capability of the vehicle are not only beneficial to the driver and passengers, but to other road users as well. We have only to compare vehicles of today with those of a decade or so ago. For example, the power produced from the engine of a family saloon car today and its maximum speed capacity, was a dream to F1 drivers of years gone by. The improvement in vehicle design and construction, together with the improvements to the interior and the additional safety equipment that is installed in various models, help to make motoring safer and more enjoyable.

Unfortunately there are new vehicles purchased by people who, being aware of the additional safety features incorporated within the vehicles, are at times inclined to abuse the vehicle or be overconfident in the way they drive. Not having the experience to handle the vehicle in the manner in which it is being driven, or by pushing the vehicle beyond its designed intention, disaster for the driver or an innocent party frequently occurs. Some drivers are under the misconception that, for example, the tyres fitted to vehicles being driven will get them out of trouble if the need should arise, regardless of the condition of the road surface or the road speed of the vehicle at the time. It must be borne in mind that the condition of the road surface dictates the stopping distance of a motor vehicle and not the tyres. This is, however, contrary to popular belief. A vehicle, however expensive or inexpensive it may be, is only as safe as the people who drive it.

There are some road users whose consideration and responsibility towards other road users leaves something to be desired. Some people purchase a particular vehicle to promote a self-image, or have personalised number plates or personalise their existing vehicle with a special colour scheme.

The 'bolt-on-goody' brigade and image-seekers who fix superfluous bits and pieces to their vehicles, often drive the vehicle in a manner that can only be described as dangerous. In their opinion they cannot see anything wrong with their driving, which makes the situation even more serious.

Numerous governments have updated and introduced new legislation for the road user, in the interest of road safety. Some members of the public disagree with many of the new laws, but if complied with at all times they will give benefit to everybody.

Furthermore, roads are being constructed using new technology and materials so that the surface will assist tyres to obtain better adhesion in most weather conditions; this is complemented by improved 'street furniture' which is being placed so that it does not obscure a driver's view, particularly at junctions. A good example is improved replacement lamp posts, this light illuminates the road in all types of weathers, at any time of day or night, thereby assisting to make our roads safer to use.

3 Road Safety

Road Safety is based on the three 'Es' of Education, Engineering and Enforcement.

Education

Teaching of road safety should begin when a child starts to walk, by being guided by the parents, who hold the child's hand or use reins. Once at First and Middle Schools the child should gain knowledge in general road safety studies.

Below:
This underpass on the A40 assists the flow of traffic and reduces the risk of accidents.

In the London Boroughs and in the Shires in the UK, road safety is implemented by Road Safety Officers with the assistance of the teaching staff of local schools. The learning of the Green Cross Code throughout the young life of the child is of paramount importance, while the first principles of Roadcraft are taught when cycle and later moped training is undertaken. The experience and knowledge gained from their training will assist when the time arrives to learn to drive a motor car.

After passing the 'L' Driving Test, the newly qualified driver who continues to practice what has been learned in the past, assisted by professional instruction, will in time be eligible to take the Advanced Driving Test. To acquire further instruction, contact your local Road Safety Officer (at the town hall or civic centre in the area where you live), who will put you in touch with organisers of 'Better Driving' classes, a 'Local Members group' or a Driving Instructor who is on the register of Advanced Driving Instructors at the Department of Transport.

It has been the norm for many years for a novice driver to be taught to drive on a one-to-one ratio. The trend today by many training establishments is to give group instruction, whereby one student is behind the wheel and those in the rear of the vehicle are drawn into the instruction, thus gaining maximum learning.

Engineering

Throughout the history of Britain, people have had to travel from one place to another, for whatever reason. As the quality of roads has improved, so has the transport using the roads. Today, with our numerous motorways, the freedom and ease of travel from one part of the country to another is taken for granted, and at times abused, by the majority of drivers of all categories of vehicles. Some arrive safely at their destination; some do not. During recent years, road engineering has improved in many ways, from new types of road surface to the design and construction of road junctions, bigger and therefore clearer traffic signs, and more well defined road markings. All of these assist in making the road user's journey easier and as safe as reasonably possible. For example, at a complex junction, where traffic is entering from numerous directions, there is potential danger at all times. To alleviate the risk of accidents and to assist traffic flow, roundabouts, flyovers or underpasses have been constructed where two primary routes cross, or where a junction has a high-density traffic flow converging.

Regardless of the cost and effort which the authorities have put into the area of need to improve our roads, unless road users change their attitude to the manner in which they drive/ride, all the engineering progress that has been made will be in vain. Inevitably, considering the volume of traffic on the roads, fatal accidents can occur for one reason or another. To alleviate the possibility of an accident, the advice given in the *Highway Code* must be complied at all times.

Enforcement

Striving for the prevention of road accidents are the police motor patrols and accident prevention units. The continued supervision and observation of the behaviour of all classes of road user helps to improve the standard of driving, through giving advice and providing assistance as and when needed. When all means of persuasion have failed, enforcement by the due process of the law is employed to uphold the road traffic legislation.

Speed in itself is not dangerous, but if used at the wrong time or in the wrong place it is lethal. It is, therefore, the biggest cause of serious road accidents. Thus there are highly specialised Traffic Patrol Officers, who are assisted in their duties of accident prevention by sophisticated aids fitted or carried in their vehicles.

The reports from traffic officers show that an increasing number of road traffic accidents are caused by excessive speed, particularly in built up areas. Vehicles involved in these accidents tend to be more severely damaged, and it often takes half an hour or more to free people trapped in a car.

New Driving Offences and Penalties

As from 1 July 1992 a range of new road safety measures came into force. The measures which are set out in the Road Traffic Act 1991, include:

- the new offences of dangerous driving and causing death by dangerous driving;

Left:
These well-defined road markings are made from reflectorised paint and glass beads (ballontini). Such road markings assist drivers to plan their driving well ahead.

Below left:
Speed reducing measures (Traffic Calming) are being used to assist the enforcement of speed limits in built-up areas. Speed humps, used in conjunction with a width restriction, are being used in this road in London.

- extended driving test for those convicted of dangerous driving;
- the new offence of causing death by careless driving when under the influence of drink or drugs;
- rehabilitation courses for drink-drivers;
- measures to facilitate the use of camera technology to detect speeding and traffic light offences;

- provisions to enable the introduction of variable speed limits (eg outside schools) and the authorised use of non-standard road humps;
- extension of the powers to prohibit unsafe motor vehicles;
- and various changes to the penalties for road traffic offences, including up to six months imprisonment for the 'hit and run' drivers, and the possible disqualification after just two speeding offences.

Road Traffic Act 1991:

New or Revised Offence	*Penalties*
● Causing death by Dangerous Driving	Maximum: 10 years imprisonment; Minimum two years disqualification; Retest; Unlimited Fine.
● Causing Death by Careless Driving Under Influence of Drink or Drugs	Maximum: Five years imprisonment; Minimum: two years disqualification; Unlimited Fine.
● Dangerous Driving	*On Indictment (Trial by Jury)* Maximum: 2 years imprisonment; Minimum: 12 months disqualification; Retest; Unlimited Fine. *Summarily (Magistrates Court)* Maximum: six months imprisonment; Minimum: 12 months disqualification; Retest; Level 5 Fine.
● Causing Danger to Road Users	Maximum: seven years imprisonment; Unlimited Fine; (six months imprisonment and/or Level 5 in Magistrates Court).
● Failing to Stop after or to Report an Accident	Maximum: six months imprisonment; Level 5 Fine; Discretionary disqualification or eight to 10 penalty points.
● Driving Without Insurance	Maximum: Level 5 Fine; Discretionary disqualification or six to eight penalty points.
● Speeding	Maximum: Level 3 Fine; Discretionary disqualification or three to six penalty points. Minimum: Fixed Penalty £32 and three penalty points.
● Failing to Identify Driver	Maximum: Level 3 Fine; three penalty points

Below:
The Police officer is using a Muni Quip T3 hand-held speed detector, which can accurately measure speeds up to 199mph.

Maximum Standard Levels of Fine are
At Present (as increased 1 October 1992 following Criminal Justice Act 1991)

- Level 1 — £200
- Level 2 — £500
- Level 3 — £1,000
- Level 4 — £2,500
- Level 5 — £5,000

To give some idea of when new equipment and traffic management measures were introduced, the following are just some examples of interest. In May 1957, police in London were given powers to remove obstructive and dangerously parked vehicles from the streets. In July 1958 the parking meter system and radar speed meters were introduced; cameras were fitted behind the windscreen of traffic patrol cars in order to take photographs of dangerous and careless driving incidents as they happened. Today video cameras are used.

Thirty-nine traffic wardens started duty in Westminster, London, in September 1960, and in 1964, box markings at road junctions and the 'Give Way' rule at roundabouts were introduced. Today, the use of camera technology to deter speeding and traffic light offences are being used, also high speed weigh-in-motion road sensors (WIMs) are being used to detect overloaded lorries. The sensors have supporting equipment which records the speed and axle/gross weights of vehicles travelling over the sensor. This is an ongoing process in which new technology is being introduced to assist the police to enforce the law.

The law Concerning Accidents

Should an accident occur on the road and involve personal injury to another person, vehicle or property, the driver must comply with the law:

Accidents

If in any case, owing to the presence of a motor vehicle on the road, an accident occurs whereby personal injury is caused to a person other than the driver of that vehicle, or damage is caused to a vehicle other than that motor vehicle, or a trailer drawn there by, or to an animal other than an animal in or on that motor vehicle or a trailer drawn thereby, the driver of the motor vehicle shall stop and, if requested to do so by any person having reasonable grounds for so requiring, give his/her name and address, and also the name and address of the owner and the identification marks of the vehicle. If for any reason he/she does not so give his/her name and address to any such person, such driver shall report the accident at a police station or to a police constable as soon as reasonably practicable and in any case within 24hr of the accident. Failure to comply with this is an offence.

Driver to produce insurance certificate or report 'injury' accidents

If in any case where owing to the presence on a road of a motor vehicle (other than an invalid carriage), an accident occurs involving personal injury to another person, and the driver of the vehicle does not at the time produce a certificate of insurance or security or other evidence to a police constable or some person who, having reasonable grounds for so doing, has required its production, the driver shall, as soon as possible, and in any case within 24hr, report the accident at a police station or to a police constable and produce his/her 'certificate'.

Failure to do so is an offence; however, he/she will not be convicted by reason only of a failure to produce his/her 'certificate' if within seven days of the accident he/she produces it in person at a police station specified by him/her at the time the accident was reported. The owner of a motor vehicle is bound to give such information as may be required by, or on behalf of, a chief officer of police, for the purpose of determining whether the use of the vehicle was, or was not, properly insured on any occasion when the driver was bound, under this section, to produce his/her certificate. Failure to do so is an offence. 'Owner' in relation to a vehicle which is the subject of a hiring agreement includes each party to the agreement.

The definition of an accident is 'an unexpected happening, having an adverse physical effect'.

We can endeavour to cost a road accident but never put a true price on it, as each accident varies in severity and quality. We can cost some of the material things which are damaged, or damaged beyond repair in an accident. The cost of a human life or the pain, suffering and grief which some casualties bear at and after a road accident, can never be accurately priced, only estimated.

The cost of a Road Accident

The Department of Transport's Highways Economic Note No 1 *Road Accidents Costs 1990*, provided estimates of the cost of road casualties and road accidents of various types.

1990 Average cost per Casualty
(All Classes of road user) by severity in £s

- Fatality £664,940
- Serious casualty £ 20,160
- Slight casualty £ 410
- Average, all casualties £ 14,070

1990 Average cost per Casualty by Class of road user in £s

- Pedestrians £24,240
- Pedal Cyclist £10,100
- Bus and Coach occupants £ 3,220
- Goods vehicle occupants £13,220
- Car and taxi occupants £11,450
- Motorised two-wheeler riders and passengers £16,920

Right:
You have been warned, take the advice seriously. *DO NOT DRINK, USE DRUGS AND DRIVE*.

- All motor vehicle road users £12,070
- Average, all road users £14,070

Note that because some elements of accident costs are not quantified, total accident costs may be regarded as minimum estimates. The variation in cost between classes or road user is due to differences in proportions of fatal, serious and slight casualties among each class of road user.

As mentioned previously, if all road users — including pedestrians — were to concentrate, anticipate and be more patient, the accident rate would be reduced. The money cost of accidents could be saved and put to uses which would benefit the community.

The Government in 1987 set a national target of reducing road casualties by one-third from 1981-85 average, by the year 2000. Thus we must all make a personal effort, otherwise the objective cannot be achieved.

Drink/Drug motoring offences

To deter the motoring public from drinking and driving, the Breathalyser was introduced in May 1967. In the first year of its use, 9,460 motorists in England and Wales were found guilty by the courts. In 1989, over 114,347 motorists in England and Wales were found guilty, as charged, of driving a motor vehicle whilst under the influence of drink/drugs.

The number of convictions for drink/drugs motoring offences is rising each year. There are some people who still 'drink and drive', thereby putting their own safety and that of others in danger, hence the severity of the punishment awarded by the convicting courts.

The Metropolitan Police

Professional training is essential in any occupation, if a high standard of competence is to be reached and continual use of the knowledge gained assists in achieving the best results at all times. By the end of 1933 the Metropolitan Police had 585 motor vehicles in use. As their fleet of vehicles increased, so did the accident rate, to one accident per 8,000 miles, due to the inadequate standard of driver training facilities. For this reason the Metropolitan Police Motor Driving School at Hendon was founded on 7 January 1935. Over the years the school has achieved its objective; to find out how it made such a contribution to road safety, let us have a look at the history of the Traffic Department and Driver Training of The Metropolitan Police, as there is much one can learn from it.

4 Metropolitan Police Driver Training

For over 50 years the Metropolitan Police Motor Driving School has been in existence. 'Hendon Trained' is an expression coined many years ago by the popular press to describe a new standard in driving which is today still a source of pride to the thousands who have passed through the School at Hendon. These students have come not only from the Metropolitan and provincial police forces, but also from countries all over the world, for such is the reputation of the School that governments of the dependencies and the Commonwealth have sent men to Hendon so that they might learn at first hand the highly skilled art of driving a motor vehicle safely in all conditions.

The events which gave rise to the formation of the Driving School are founded in the more leisurely past, when the gas-lit streets of Victorian London echoed to the clip-clop of horse's hooves as the 'growlers' and broughams made their sedate way through the West End. The motor car was then a dream, and the sole means of motive power, the horse.

It was in 1758 that law enforcement officers, realising the need for mobility, purchased two horses for the police office at Bow Street. Horses have played an essential part in mobility ever since; in Central London during the middle part of the last century, each major police station had its stables from which mounted officers went out daily to patrol their beats. In the then rural extremities of the Metropolitan Police area mounted officers operated from Horse Patrol Stations, patrolling the main coaching roads in much the same way as their present-day colleagues who operate from District Garages.

Probably the first police vehicle was the horse-drawn prison van, a reference to which is made in Police Orders of 1858. These were the Black Marias, so named after Maria Lee, a giant Boston negress whose size and strength was such that when the constables required assistance it was a common thing to send for Maria, who quickly dealt with the trouble makers and marched them off to the lock-up. Today, although the term is extended to all police vans, surprisingly few people are aware of its transatlantic origin.

The Motor Car Act of 1903 was the first statute which applied specifically to the internal combustion engine. Before this, motor cars were governed by legislation which was intended for steam propelled vehicles. Those motor cars which were in being prior to 1898 were subject to the provisions of the Locomotives Act of 1865, which regulated the 'use of locomotives on turnpike and local roads'. This, in effect,. meant that every motor car had to be preceded by a man on foot waving a red flag. With the passing of the 1903 Act the motor car, rather belatedly, received its emancipation.

It was in this year that two 7½hp Wolseley touring cars were purchased, for use by the Commissioner and the Receiver, who then, as now, was responsible for administering the finances of the Force. The registration marks allotted to these vehicles, A 209 and A 210, are still associated with the police. A 209 has been retained by the Receiver for his official car, and A 210 for use by the Home Secretary, the Minister answerable to Parliament as the responsible authority for the Metropolitan Police.

As the motor car became the established successor to the horse as a means of transport, so the scope of its commercial use increased, and it was not long before the London criminals realised its potential. Thus was born the 'smash and grab' raid. By 1920 these raids had reached such serious proportions that the Commissioner of the day introduced a new and revolutionary method of policing. The main reason for the success achieved by criminals in this new type of crime was the fact that the police were greatly handicapped by the lack of transport. Not only could the criminal choose the time and place for the raid, but by using a motor vehicle he was almost assured of a complete getaway. In an endeavour to combat this new threat to law and order, four Crossley tenders were made available for the formation of a special squad. Volunteers were called for from PCs in Divisions with driving experience, and after a driving test these officers (together with specially selected detectives) were formed into teams as mobile crime patrols. Working in plain clothes, from the seemingly innocent tenders.

Prior to 1932, police drivers were selected from members of the Force with driving experience who possessed sufficient technical knowledge to carry out minor repairs. There was no system of grading according to ability. By 1932, however, due to the expansion of the transport fleet and the increasing variety of vehicles in use, a system of grading was introduced. Although undoubtedly a step in the right direction, it made no provision for instruction or progressive training, but it was at least a sign of the growing awareness within the Force that ultimately it would be necessary to provide some form of training for the drivers of this fast-growing fleet of vehicles.

1932 provided yet another step forward in the history of police transport, for it was in this year that the 'Box System' was introduced. Briefly, this system consisted of the erection of the familiar blue telephone box (immortalised by *Dr Who*) or post on or near every beat as a means of direct communication with the local Sub-Divisional station, by both the patrolling constable and members of the public.

By the end of 1933 the number of vehicles in use by the Force had risen to 585. Unfortunately, as the fleet grew in size, so the number of accidents in which police were involved grew correspondingly, and in the first few months of 1934 the accident mileage ratio rose to one accident for every 8,000 miles. This high rate resulted in considerable adverse comment both in the Press and motoring journals, and as a result of this criticism the Commissioner, Lord Trenchard, arranged for the famous racing motorist Sir Malcolm Campbell to test a number, of drivers from Divisions. This difficult and strenuous test consisted of driving a Squad or 'Q' car on normal patrol and on an emergency (999) call, both in heavy traffic and on the open road. Despite the severity of the test and the high standard demanded, all the police drivers passed with flying colours and such was Sir Malcolm Campbell's praise that the ill-founded criticism was silenced. It could not, however, be denied that lack of experience and inadequate training facilities in particular were a great handicap in raising the standard of driving. For these reasons in 1934 the setting up of the Metropolitan Police Driving School at Hendon was ordered.

The introduction of the Driving School caused very little comment, either locally or nationally. Few could have foreseen the impact which the teaching of the School would have on driving technique, not only in this country, but in other lands throughout the world. Nevertheless, 'tall oaks from little acorns grow' and this is especially true of the Driving school, for the seed so firmly planted in 1934 has today grown into a strong tree, the branches of which stretch far and wide.

So outstanding were the results achieved from the training given to the students who attended the initial courses that the pattern of future instruction was clear. In 1936 an advance course of driving for Flying Squad, 'Q' car and Traffic Patrol car drivers was introduced, and early in 1937 the Commissioner appointed as his civilian adviser for the training of police drivers one of the most famous racing drivers of the day, the late Earl of Cottenham. The Earl, who in earlier years had been a member of both the Alvis and Sunbeam racing teams, approached his task with a rare zest. His aim was simply to bring the techniques of advanced driving to a new standard of perfection. To this end he personally trained six specially selected instructors to give this training. In this way the Advanced Car Wing was born, and Lord Cottenham's teaching laid down those many years ago still forms the whole basis of instruction for police drivers. Briefly, his system was that by implementing a simple 'drill' or sequence of events, a driver would ensure that his vehicle was always in the right place at the right time, travelling at the right speed and in the correct gear. Thus, it was reasoned, a driver would be in complete control of the car and any situation with which he might be faced. The success of Lord Cottenham's teaching can be best judged by results, for whilst in 1934 the police vehicle accident rate was one accident in every 8,000 miles, by 1938 it had dropped to one accident in every 27,000 miles.

Lord Cottenham's stay with the Metropolitan Police was brief, as he left in 1938, but the impact of his teaching remains, and the system of driving which he initiated has resulted in a police average for each blameworthy accident in 1982 of one every 26,108 miles for cars and one every 86,842 miles for motor cycles; proof, if proof was every needed, that good driving and training pays a handsome dividend in safety on the road.

The use of motor cycles in the Force has increased rapidly since the Chater-Lea combination made its brief appearance in 1924. They were found to be invaluable (as indeed they are today) for getting to the forefront of traffic jams, and their increased use, mainly by Traffic Patrols, has grown with the passing years. They are used not only as an aid in keeping London's traffic moving, but for escorting large and cumbersome loads, providing escorts for visiting Royalty and Heads of State, and enforcing the provisions of the Road Traffic Acts.

Although the Motor Cycle Wing of the Driving School was introduced in 1938, the training of motor cyclists had in fact commenced much earlier. In January 1936 a few selected Traffic Patrol officers were tested as to their suitability to ride motor cycles, and these tests subsequently developed into two-day courses. These short courses soon exposed the need for fuller training, and so the Motor Cycle Wing was added to the Standard and Advanced Wings as an integral part of the School.

One of the first postwar tasks undertaken by the Driving School was the training of a number of Ministry of Transport driving test examiners. These examiners were given a special two-week course with the Advanced Wing, so that in carrying out their important task of testing members of the public, they would have at least themselves have the best possible yardstick with which to measure the standard of others.

Unfortunately the task of training all the Ministry examiners was too big for the School to undertake in addition to its normal commitments, and eventually the Ministry of Transport had, of necessity, to institute its own training programme.

Since the introduction of Traffic Patrols in 1930, their work has increased enormously with each succeeding year. As more and more vehicles poured on to already inadequate roads, and new types with a variety of technical improvements left the factories annually, traffic legislation rapidly reached a state where some form of specialist study was needed to enable the Traffic Patrols to carry out their work efficiently. In order to provide training in this specialised field, the Traffic Patrol Wing was introduced in 1948.

Its initial task was to give preliminary instruction to officers selected for Traffic Patrol duty. Later, in 1959, an advanced level course was organised for the older, more experienced officers to fit them for operating the specially equipped traffic accident cars. Both courses are still in being. They are constantly being revised to keep pace with the ever increasing complexity of the traffic problem in the metropolis, and the comprehensive instruction given to students attending the Traffic Patrol Wing provides a firm foundation for the many and varied daily duties which the Traffic Patrols are required to carry out.

During the Earl of Cottenham's term of office at the School, the method of teaching on both Car Wings was standardised. so that all students had the same curriculum. Each instructor possessed his own set of duplicated notes, and the students were required to copy out pages and pages of notes covering each phase of instruction — a laborious process. In 1955, however, it was decided that the teaching of the School might well benefit the general motoring public, and so the sheaf of typewritten notes used so effectively by countless instructors was edited and printed by Her Majesty's Stationary Office.

It appeared as *Roadcraft*, on which this book *Advanced Driving* is based. Almost overnight it became a best seller. *Roadcraft*, and its sister publication, the *Highway Code*, are the books which form the basis of every police driver's training, and the motorist who reads these books in conjunction with *Advanced Driving* and the *Illustrated Highway Code*, understands and acts upon the advice and instruction given therein is well on the way to becoming a good driver.

On completing the Standard Car Course, students were returned to Divisions to gain practical experience, and after completing some 15,000 to 20,000 miles they were eligible to be tested as to their suitability for an Advanced Course. In very many cases the sudden transition from the low-powered general purpose cars and vans on which the driver had gained his/her experience to the high-powered cars of the Advanced Wing was too much, and so in 1957 the Intermediate Course was introduced. Of two weeks duration, this course provided a 'half way' stage at which students received instruction in driving medium-powered cars. Drivers who successfully completed this Intermediate Course were returned to Divisions to gain further experienced prior to an Advanced Course. They were then entitled to drive radio-equipped patrol cars, and the experience thus gained soon paid a handsome dividend in an ever higher standard of driving when students attended the Advanced Course.

The growth of the transport fleet, new methods of policing and the constant need to train police drivers to even higher standards of skills of efficiency, has increased the work of the Driving School. From those two Wolseley cars in 1903, the fleet has grown to number nearly 3,700 vehicles of all types, and the primary, but no means the only function of Driving School is to ensure that the officers who volunteer and are selected for driving duties are trained to the highest possible standard.

Driving School Today

Over and above the main courses mentioned, refresher, reclassification and special courses are held as necessary; as a result, approximately 4,500 students are trained each year. In addition, the Driving School receives over 500 visitors from all walks of life annually, and instructors are constantly in demand as lecturers at schools, motor and motorcycle clubs and business organisations.

Metropolitan Police teams have also entered the highly competitive field of rallying, and competitions are entered against the Army MT school, in such events as 'Copdrive'. Motorcyclists from the School, Traffic Patrol and Districts compete each year in the Services, Scottish six-day and other such trails with a good deal of success — all of them 'Hendon trained'.

So we have moved from the past to the present, from the horse-drawn Black Marias of 1858 to the power-packed vehicles of today. For nearly 60 years the Metropolitan Police Driving School has occupied its place as a world leader in driver training and its methods have been adopted and copied throughout the world. Graduates from the School are scattered in their thousands, not only in Metropolitan London but all over the civilised world. To all of them 'Hendon' means something more than a dot on the map. It evokes, in each and every one of them, a blend of nostalgia and inner pride, for wherever motorists gather or motoring is discussed the expression 'Hendon trained' still stands for all that is best in driving.

The School motto is *Experientia Docet — Experience Teaches* — and may it always be passed on.

It must be appreciated that during the time the Earl of Cottenham was at Hendon, instructors from Chelmsford (Essex) and Hutton (Lancs) were taught the System of Car Control by him, therefore the three original Police Driving Schools in the United Kingdom — Hendon, Chelmsford and Hutton — were Home Office Approved.

Today there are 47 Home Office Approved Police Motor Driving Schools, of which 15 are approved at Advanced Level the remaining 32 are Standard Level only.

Right:
Chapter 17 deals with driving through water.

5 Car Control

Of the three contributory factors to the cause of a road accident, human error and the presence of a human being is directly responsible for almost every one. Young male drivers in the 17-21 year old group are widely regarded as 'unsafe' due to the image some of them portray — flash/macho — while driving a motor vehicle. Many of the young people in this age group who have a full driving licence have been classed as 'throttle jockeys' and not drivers. This can be said of some people of an older age group too. Much has to be done to change the irresponsible attitude that some people have when driving a motor vehicle. The Police System of Car Control as devised many years ago by the Earl of Cottenham is a system or drill, each feature of which is considered, in sequence, by the driver at the approach to any hazard. It is the basis upon which the whole technique of good driving is built.

The System of Car Control creates a simpie and repetitive method of driving which ensures that the driver omits no detail, leaves nothing to chance and when perfected gives that one crucial ingredient essential to safe driving — TIME TO REACT.

If the drivers of the cars in the accompanying illustrations had been in the right place on the road at the right time, travelling at the right speed and in the correct gear, they would have been in complete control, but as can be seen they were not.

Before going on to the System of Car Control, there are numerous aspects and characteristics of a vehicle which should be known by the driver. These have often been ignored, and when a vehicle is being driven fast by a driver who has not accustomed himself to the controls, especially the acceleration and braking capabilities, a potentially dangerous situation could occur.

Far left:
The driver of this car appears to have committed two serious errors. (1) For an unknown reason the roundabout was not seen; possibly this was due to lack of concentration.

Left:
And, (2) the speed on the approach was probably too fast. The consequent result can be seen.

Right:
A driver took a short cut over this roundabout. In doing so he has demolished a traffic sign, which was there to assist him.

Far right:
The driver of this car did not take the condition of the road surface into consideration, before applying too much acceleration on leaving a roundabout.

Below right:
The driver's back should be well supported by the seat and the left leg should be comfortable when the clutch pedal is pressed fully down. The driver's hands should be placed naturally with the palms on the rim of the wheel, fingers should fold around the rim resting lightly but ready to grip when necessary.

Far right:
Elbows must not be placed on the window frame, arm rests, etc, because this reduces control. On slippery roads, any steering movements should be delicate, otherwise skids may be induced. Hands should be placed on the wheel in the 'ten to two' but no lower than a 'quarter to three' position. The wheel should not be gripped tightly, but ready to exert maximum leverage if necessary. The driver should not cross his hands when turning the wheel, as precise control cannot be obtained.

Driving Position

The driver should be in control of the vehicle at all times. One factor enabling the driver to achieve this is the position in which the driver sits whilst driving. There are some drivers who slouch in the driving seat or sit too close to the steering wheel. There are others who sit too far back, seat partially reclined and with arms fully extended, and have difficulty operating the foot pedals and hand controls properly — often imitating the style of their heroes in the world of motor sport, a method which is not suitable on the public highway.

The ideal seating position must be found to suit the stature of the individual driver. If practically possible the driving seat should be adjusted so that the pedals can be operated without fuss and without discomfort, and so that hand controls and auxiliary switches are within easy reach. The driver should sit upright and alert, not taut or strained, yet not too relaxed.

The steering characteristics built in as a design feature in one make of car may not be included in another, thus steering may be light in one car and heavy in another. This emphasises that, whilst each car may be outwardly similar, detail differences do exist and should be taken into account when selecting the optimum driving position.

Steering

The vehicle may respond more (oversteer) or less (understeer) than the driver expects; alternatively the steering may be or may not be power assisted. The driver must quickly adapt himself to the feel of the vehicle being driven, so that he is able to place it where he wants, in all conditions.

Both hands should remain on the wheel unless it is necessary to remove one or other to signal, operate an auxiliary switch or to change gear, etc. Any change from the straight course must be actioned gradually and smoothly, other than when manoeuvring at slow speeds. The steering wheel should be turned by the 'pull and push' method as shown in the accompanying diagram. Most vehicles have steering which is self-straightening and control will be necessary to prevent the steering wheel from spinning back; spinning back represents lazy driving and is potentially dangerous.

Accordingly, the steering wheel should be fed back by hand movements, in the reverse order to which it was originally turned.

Road Surfaces and Tyre Care

The majority of drivers are not aware of the condition or type of road surface they drive on. But they soon complain about a slippery road surface after a skid has occurred. The Advanced Driver, who looks well ahead, thus recognising any change and condition of road surface in good time, will appreciate and apply the correct levels of braking, acceleration, steering and road speed on the approach to bends, junctions and other hazards, so that maximum road holding is always achieved.

The majority of road surfaces when clean and dry are good or fairly good for road holding. When the weather is wet, the road surface can become slippery; more so during a shower of rain following a long spell of dry weather, when rubber dust and oil get washed to the road surface, which cause tyres to lose adhesion. The presence of ice, frost, snow, mud and wet leaves each has its own distinctive appearance, and must not be ignored, because they too are factors that can cause tyres to lose adhesion, thereby affecting control of the vehicle.

It must be borne in mind that during wintry weather, road surfaces become frosty and ice-covered, more so on bridges and flyovers because of the cold air flowing beneath them. A good driver, who looks well ahead, recognises any change in road surface through its colour or its feel through the steering wheel. The driver should also be aware of the danger from any area of road that is shaded, because ice could be present. In these circumstances he/she must take due precautions in good time and apply the correct levels of braking, acceleration and steering so that maximum

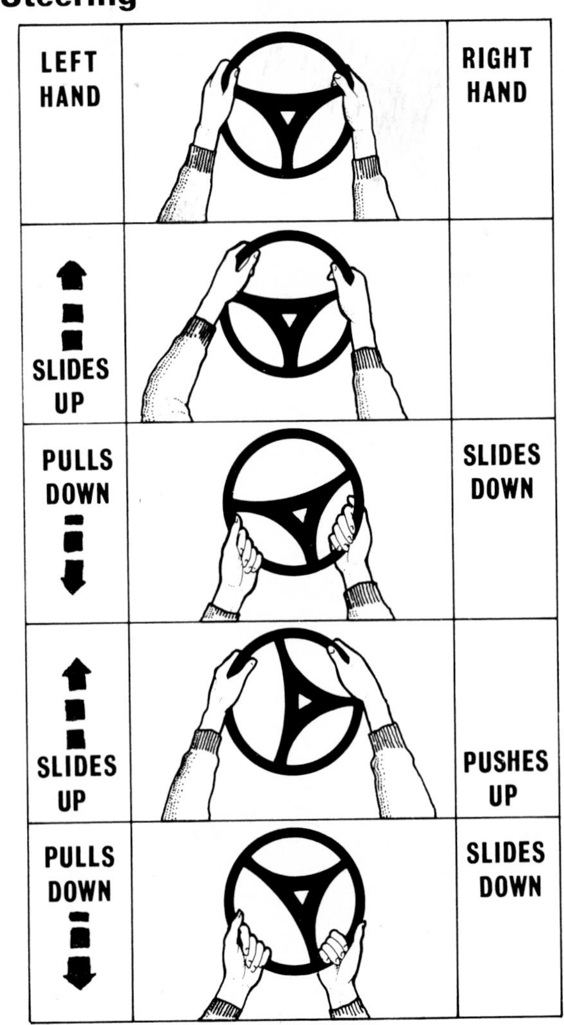

Figure 2
Steering
The accompanying diagram illustrates hand and steering movements for turning left. For a turn to the right the first steering movement will be the right hand pulling down from the 12 o'clock position.

Right:
The sign warns the driver of the possibility of side wind that could blow the vehicle off course. The driver should make himself aware of which direction the wind is blowing, and be prepared to take a firmer grip on the steering wheel if necessary.

Far right:
Grooves in the road surface can have the same effect as being on tram lines. They should, therefore, be avoided if possible.

Below right:
When wet leaves are present speed should be reduced well before reaching the hazard.

Far right:
Mud on the road can have the same effect on tyre adhesion as that of ice.

Far left:
The braking distance should be trebled when braking on a slippery surface like wet cobblestones, ice, mud and wet leaves. Skidding will be induced by any sudden and harsh use of the controls. Therefore, the driver's focal point of concentration should be projected further ahead.

Left:
Ice can be seen in the middle and nearside edge of the road. A motorcyclist could not have recognised its presence; the consequent result is all too apparent.

Below left:
Ice can be seen in the shaded area. Should an approaching driver not realise ice is present, a dangerous situation could occur.

road holding is always achieved to avoid skidding. It should be borne in mind that tyres travelling on ice make virtually no noise.

The good driver will also look out for deep potholes, projecting manhole covers, sunken gullies and any other objects likely to damage tyres. A deep pothole, if ignored while travelling at speed round a bend, could cause the driver to lose effective steering control (course) and the rear of the vehicle could start tramping round the bend, which could have disastrous consequences. When intending to park the vehicle on the road, the driver should bring the vehicle to rest in a safe place and position, close to and parallel with the kerb yet avoiding tyre contact with it, thus preventing damage to the tyre(s).

Acceleration

Each year, vehicle manufacturers spend vast sums of money designing vehicles for the future. However, the benefits of sleek aerodynamic-shaped cars that have low drag factors, which assist the driver to achieve high mileage for the minimum of fuel used, are often wasted by the driver using the accelerator incorrectly (at the wrong time and place). There are some drivers who are unaware of the fact that the performance capabilities of different vehicles vary considerably according to the efficiency of the engine and power-to-weight ratio: they purchase a family saloon car expecting — and demanding — the same performance as a very special high powered sports car — often with fatal results, as statistics prove.

The term 'acceleration' in this context means that, when pressure is exerted on the accelerator pedal, the road/engine speed of the motor vehicle will increase. Acceleration affects the behaviour of a vehicle as it travels along the road, more so when moving off from a stationary position. It is either pushed along (rear-wheel drive), pulled along (front-wheel drive) or pulled and pushed at the same time (four-wheel drive). These different types of transmission have their own distinctive influence on the stability of the vehicle. When hard pressure is suddenly applied on the accelerator, it will induce wheel spin, then skidding (more so on a slippery road surface), and finally cause the vehicle to drive through a curved path; therefore heavy acceleration when a low gear is selected should be avoided if tyre adhesion with the road is to be maintained. For these reasons it is desirable that hard acceleration is applied only when the vehicle is travelling in a straight line, because the vehicle is most stable when the weight is evenly distributed.

Weight Transfer Under Acceleration

The instant a car accelerates, a proportion of its mass is transferred from the front to the rear wheels (see Figure 3). The phenomenon has no effect on steering, but grip at the rear is increased. This explains the superiority of rear-wheel drive cars when it comes to transmitting high power outputs to the road. Conversely, a front-wheel drive car is penalised under acceleration. The load on its driven wheels is reduced and torque is less efficiently transmitted to the ground.

The rear-wheel drive car on the other hand, benefits a sort of spiral effect. The harder a driver accelerates, the more weight is transferred to the rear wheels and the more power is efficiently transmitted to the road. There is, of course, a limit.

It is therefore of the utmost importance that a thorough understanding of the accelerator, gears, brakes and steering is essential. With intelligent use of these controls the System of Car Control can be developed. It is surprising, but true, that many drivers are unaware that they misuse the accelerator until they receive professional driving instruction to improve their skill. A good driver will use the accelerator precisely at the right time and place, avoiding sudden and coarse movements which result in uneven and thus jerky vehicle control. It should be borne in mind that speed may be reduced by deceleration when the pressure on the pedal is eased; the engine will slow down due to the compression in the cylinders, and thus slowing down will be transmitted to the driving wheels. As engine-induced deceleration is a gradual process, it will have little effect on the adhesion of the tyres on the road. The loss of road speed by engine deceleration will also be more effective when a low gear is engaged. This should be borne in mind when driving on roads that have a slippery surface when normal braking could induce skidding, and to assist braking when descending steep hills. A driver is advised to wear footwear that is light in weight, preferably shoes, because thick-soled, heavy boots will restrict the sensation of pedal movement.

Figure 3
Weight transfer under acceleration.

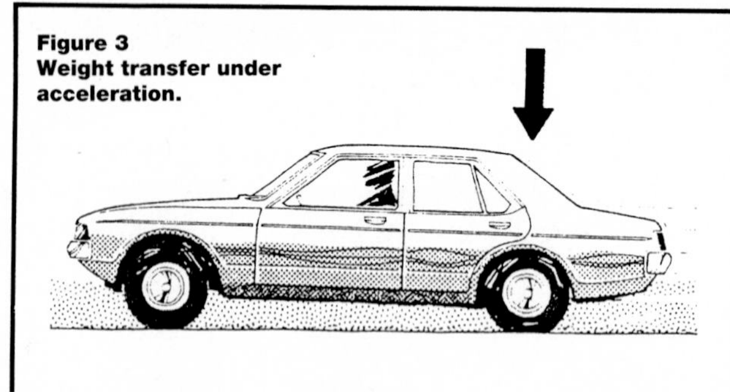

Acceleration Sense

The object of Feature Six in the System of Car Control is to consider and apply the correct degree of acceleration required for the turn and exit for the hazard so that it can be completed safely, with due regard for the type of road surface, the actual and potential presence of other vehicles and pedestrians, the speed that is safe to travel for the conditions prevailing at the time. For these reasons the vehicle should be travelling in the right place on the road, at the right speed, and with the correct gear engaged. In so doing, it will be contributing to the driver's safety in certain potentially dangerous situations. It will also be possible to accelerate out of danger as well as to brake, bearing in mind that in particular situations

Left:

Closing Gap

When the road ahead cannot be seen to be clear an Advanced Driver, who is catching up with a slower vehicle, will have eased off the accelerator in good time, thereby using deceleration as a brake. At the same time he will be in a correct position to overtake when the road ahead can be seen to be clear.

Below left:

This driver has caught up with a slower vehicle which cannot be overtaken due to approaching traffic. The driver kept his foot on the accelerator too long, due to lack of acceleration sense, and is therefore, having to brake hard to reduce his excess speed.

braking could result in stopping in the path of approaching danger, when acceleration would have enabled the driver to avoid the danger.

Acceleration sense can be applied to every facet of driving. There are many drivers who do not combine observation with acceleration sense, eg maintaining a constant speed when catching a slower moving vehicle, then find it necessary to brake hard; or, on leaving a hazard, applying hard pressure on the accelerator when it is obvious that there is a traffic hold-up ahead. A skilled driver will act on the information gained by good powers of observation (looking and planning well ahead), in doing so will drive with efficiency and with the minimum wear to the vehicle.

Braking

Many drivers drive at a speed well outside the bounds of safety for the prevailing conditions, unaware of the state or type of road surface. It is easy to recognise the fault after the event has occurred. In normal driving conditions, primary braking must be by proper use of the brake and not by using the gears. For all normal braking the initial free movement of the pedal should be taken up gently and pressure progressively increased as necessary until it can be relaxed as the unwanted road speed is lost. When braking to a standstill the final effort should be so judged that the vehicle is brought to a gliding halt without jerking or suddenly settling down at the rear end.

TABLE 1

From the moment the driver applies the brake to the time the vehicle comes to rest is called the braking or stopping distance. The average driver takes 0.7sec from seeing an emergency situation to placing his foot on the brake pedal.

THINKING DISTANCE at 30mph

Distance travelled during reaction time

Time (sec)	*Distance* (ft/m)	*Time* (sec)	*Distance* (ft/m)
.175	7.7/2.3	.475	20.9/6.3
.2	8.8/2.7	.5	22/6.7
.225	9.9/3.0	.525	23.1/7.0
.25	11/3.3	.55	24.2/7.3
.275	12.1/3.7	.575	25.3/7.7
.3	13.2/4.0	.6	26.4/8.0
.325	14.3/4.3	.625	27.5/8.3
.35	15.4/4.7	.65	28.6/8.7
.375	16.5/5.0	.675	29.7/9.0
.4	17.6/5.3	.7	30.8/9.3
.425	18.7/5.7	.725	31.9/9.7
.45	19.8/6.0	.75	33/10.0

REMEMBER — This does *not* include braking distance which at 30mph is a further 45ft.

TOTAL STOPPING DISTANCE

Distance travelled assuming an about average reaction time

Speed (mph)	*Reaction Distance* (ft/m)	*Braking Distance* (ft/m)	*Total Stopping Distance* (ft/m)
20	20/6.0	20/6.0	40/12.0
30	30/9.1	45/13.6	75/22.7
40	40/12.0	80/24.0	120/36.0
50	50/15.1	125/37.9	175/53.0
60	60/18.2	180/54.6	240/73.0
70	70/21.1	245/74.2	315/95.3

REMEMBER — These braking distances only apply on *dry* road surfaces. On wet roads, they would double.

Weight Transfer Under Braking

When braking hard, weight is transferred to the front wheels. It is now their turn to benefit from superior grip. This explains why, in the interests of brake balance, the majority of a car's braking capacity is at the front. That's also why it is often the front wheels which lock first under heavy braking.

If the distribution of the braking were identical front and rear, the front wheels would never be sufficiently braked, while the rear wheels with less load, would be permanently locked. ABS prevents the locking up of wheels when heavy braking is applied.

Anti-lock braking is another example of the technology spin-off from the aerospace industry. The first application of an anti-lock braking system was probably on the B47 bomber introduced in 1947. The difference between a vehicle with ABS and one without

Figure 4
Weight transfer under braking.

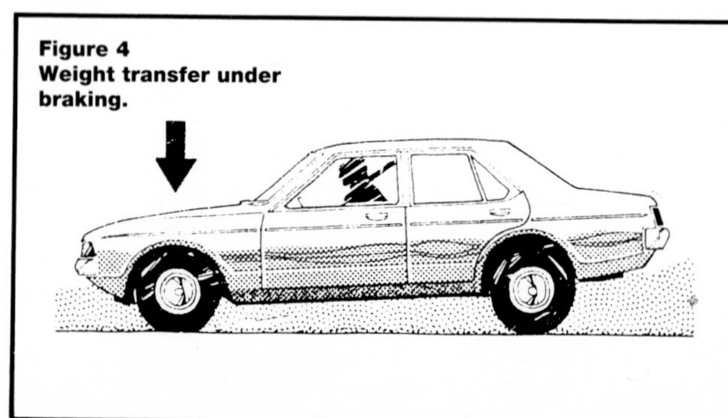

is that ABS enables a driver to stop as quickly as a given situation demands, under full control, on most types of road surface at all and not just at some times. For example, the wheels on one side of the car may be travelling on a loose surface at the side of the road, while the wheels on the other side are being braked on good dry asphalt. In this situation, no form of intermittent 'cadence' braking technique on the driver's part will help, since it can only be applied to all four wheels at the same time, whereas with ABS, the driver can be sure that only the wheels with adequate grip will transmit the braking. However, it must be borne in mind that should a driver approach a corner or enter a bend too fast or brake hard on ice, snow and mud, ABS control cannot work miracles. Unchanging physical principles govern braking. Braking is certain to take longer on a wet road than a dry one, regardless of what type of tyres are fitted to the vehicle. Drivers must avoid developing a false sense of security.

Taking the Mystery Out of ABS

There are some drivers who are aware of the term ABS but are not sure what ABS actually does, the following explains.

As a rotating wheel is braked, it passes through what engineers term a 'slip phase'. A freely rotating wheel has a zero slip, a locked and skidding wheel on the other hand has a 'slip factor' of 100%. Maximum retardation is not achieved with locked wheels, but when the wheel is in the slip phase, which may be between 10 and 30% according to the road surface and the conditions of the tyres. Every driver should know that tyre grip, and therefore braking effectiveness, is higher on a dry, coarse surface than a smooth, wet one.

Unfortunately braking is dependent on many factors which the driver can't always assess or control in an emergency; invariably, most human reactions are simply not fast enough to cope. In emergency braking one of the biggest dangers, of course, is if the front wheels lock. The car just ploughs straight on, failing to take a bend, thus skids straight ahead to hit an obstruction or other road user because there's no response to steering.

Alternatively, if the rear wheels lock, the front wheels can still be steered but the car starts to spin around its yaw axis, possibly resulting in loss of control. It has always been a golden rule of driving, never to brake hard and steer at the same time — a sure recipe for disaster because a locked wheel cannot be steered. ABS now makes it possible to retain complete steering control while applying maximum braking. It must always be borne in mind, however, that the condition of the road surface dictates the stopping distance.

A driver who looks and plans well ahead should not have to use secondary braking on the approach to a junction/hazard. For example the driver should lose all unwanted road speed by braking, except for minor variations in speed when deceleration will be sufficient. The gear selected should be appropriate to match the engine and road speed. Some drivers select an inappropriate gear then realise that the road speed is still too fast for a safe approach to the hazard, therefore have to re-apply the brake a second time, which is poor control, thus the term 'secondary braking'.

Left:
The driver did not lose all excess speed when the brake was applied. A lower gear has been engaged but the road speed is still too fast, thus the driver is having to re-apply the brake.

Right:

The advice given by the traffic sign should be complied with, the mirrors should be used so that the position and speed of any following traffic is known before the brakes are checked.

Far right:

It is of the utmost importance to carry out firm braking while travelling in a straight line.

Below right:

The driver of this car has left his braking too late, therefore could lose control.

Apart from other considerations, the speed of a vehicle at any time must not exceed the speed at which it can be stopped within the distance the driver can see to be clear. The driver must know the distance he needs to slow down appreciably or stop, from all road speeds. Not only must he know the distances, but must be able to relate them to the road on which he is travelling. On a good dry road the average vehicle should be capable of stopping in the distances shown in the *Highway Code*.

Reaction time may be defined as the time that passes between the moment the driver observes the need to apply the brake and the moment he takes that action. The average driver takes 0.7sec from seeing an emergency situation to placing his foot on the brake pedal. The distance covered in that time is known as the 'thinking distance' and will be the same figure in feet as the speed in mph, eg 30mph=30ft (9m). Thinking distance+braking distance=stopping distance.

The thinking distance will vary in four ways:

- (a) the speed at which the vehicle is travelling;
- (b) the physical and mental condition of the driver;
- (c) the degree of concentration being applied at the time;
- (d) The road that can and cannot be seen to be clear at the time.

Controlled, firm braking is most effective when the wheel is still revolving just before the point of locking, which is preferable to a sudden hard application on the brake pedal which will induce the vehicle to skid, more so when the road surface is wet. To maintain stability of the car, and equal distribution of weight while braking, the following rules should be applied:

- (1) brake firmly only when travelling in a straight line;
- (2) vary brake pressure according to the condition of the road surface;
- (3) brake in good time, well before reaching the hazard;
- (4) when descending a steep winding hill, brake firmly on the straight stretches and ease off the brake in the bends. Remember the value of engaging a low gear at an early stage in the descent.

Gear Changing

No matter how well a driver may handle a vehicle, his use of the gearbox will do much to make or mar his driving. Therefore it is surprising, but true, how many drivers misuse the gears every time they drive. This could be due to lack of knowledge of gear ratios of the gearbox and its functions. One of the hallmarks of a good driver is the ability to change gear smoothly at the right time and place. Selection of the correct gear for the situation enables the driver to accelerate out of a hazard, if it is safe to do so, or be able to stop should the need arise, thereby complying with the dictates of roadcraft. At the same time use of the correct gear achieves economy and safety. The essential ingredients in changing gear correctly are the ability accurately to match engine revolutions to road speed, together with precise operation of the clutch and accelerator when using the gears.

Faults

- Braking and changing gear at the same time is a control fault. All unwanted road speed should be lost by proper use of the footbrake or deceleration, then the appropriate gear selected. A gear change should not be made in the initial stages of braking. The 'Heel and Toe method' (heel on the brake and toe on the accelerator) when braking and changing gear at the same time is not good driving while on the public highway, and can be dangerous. Therefore it should not be done.
- Moving off from stationary in second gear, creating excessive engine speed and unnecessary wear to the clutch. First gear should be used to get the vehicle over the initial stage of inertia, then a higher gear selected as appropriate. When moving off on a steep down gradient it is acceptable to start in second gear providing no undue wear occurs to the clutch and the accelerator is not used excessively.
- Selecting a lower gear to slow down instead of using the brakes, with the exception of brake failure or on a road surface that is slippery.
- Poor co-ordination between hand and foot to make a clean smooth gear change.
- Changing to a lower gear on a 'closing gap' followed by another gear change then an application of the brakes. The correct procedure is explained earlier in Acceleration Sense.
- Changing gear at the wrong time and place, eg while overtaking, or on a corner or bend. The gear should be selected on the approach to the hazard, not in it.
- When moving off, going up through the gears as quickly as possible, then having to change down again when it was obvious that an intermediate gear was suitable for the prevailing conditions.
- Going through the gears, gear by gear, when the situation justifies that intermediate gears can be by-passed, eg 4-2 or 2-4.

- Not being aware of the correct degree of acceleration needed to drive safely out of the hazard (Feature Six in the System of Car Control) due to the incorrect gear being engaged at the time. This could put the driver in a potentially dangerous situation.
- There is little to be gained in double de-clutching on a vehicle that has a synchromesh gearbox fitted, unless there is a fault with the synchromesh.

It is of paramount importance that the driver is aware of the approximate maximum and minimum road speed in each gear of the vehicle he is driving, because the correct use of gears is part of vehicle sympathy. A driver who concentrates and respects the vehicle being driven will with self-discipline and practice, change gear with delicacy and smoothness, and thus be on the way to acquiring a polished driving style, the ultimate aim of the Advanced Driver.

Gear selection faults with automatic transmission

- Failure to apply the handbrake or footbrake before engaging 'D' or 'R' when stationary. This is potentially dangerous if the choke is in use.
- Starting (if the vehicle permits) the engine in 'P' rather than 'N' which would avoid going through reverse, with a cold or high revving engine.
- Selecting a lower gear 'L' at too high a road speed.
- Moving the selector to 'N' when making temporary stops.
- Not applying the handbrake when the vehicle has stopped with a gear engaged and the footbrake not applied.
- The accelerator should never be pressed while moving the gear selector.
- When parked on a steep gradient the gear selector should be moved to 'P'=Park, thereby providing additional security should the handbrake fail. It is advisable to move the gear selector to 'N'=Neutral before starting the engine.

The Handbrake

Under normal conditions the handbrake should not be applied until the vehicle is stationary. The pawl release should be operated when the handbrake is applied, to prevent wear to the ratchet. As experience is gained, it will not be necessary to apply the hand-brake for every momentary stop. However, when the vehicle has been stopped and the intention of the driver is to leave the vehicle, the handbrake must be applied and the engine stopped. This is a

Right:

Gear Selection

On a steep down gradient a low gear should be engaged thereby using engine compression to assist in controlling the road speed of the vehicle. This avoids long periods of sustained braking that can cause brake fade.

legal requirement and must be complied with; otherwise a dangerous situation could occur, and legal proceedings could be taken.

When driving a vehicle fitted with automatic transmission the driver should be aware that the vehicle may 'creep' when stationary with the engine ticking over and the gear selector lever in 'D' or 'R' (or equivalent position). To prevent the vehicle moving unexpectedly, the handbrake should be applied. If circumstances mean the vehicle is likely to be stationary for longer than a momentary stop, neutral should be selected. When starting a cold engine and the choke is being used, the driver must check that the handbrake is applied (on) before the engine is started, as the vehicle could move off unexpectedly, with dire consequences.

Pre-Driving Check

It is surprising but true that numerous accidents are caused each year by careless drivers, who stop the engine with a gear engaged fail to apply the handbrake, and leave the vehicle. On re-entering the vehicle, the thoughtless driver makes no safety checks and turns the ignition key, in consequence the vehicle jumps forward/backward and, in doing so, collides with another vehicle or pedestrian. It is, therefore, of the utmost importance that commonsense must prevail; the driver must take all necessary safety precautions before leaving the vehicle and before restarting the engine. Should an unfamiliar vehicle have to be driven, the driver must accustom himself with the position and operation of all the controls, before the vehicle is moved.

Before starting the engine the driver must make sure it is safe to do so, therefore the following routine should be carried out:

- (a) Make sure the handbrake is on.
- (b) Check that the gear lever is in neutral.
- (c) Adjust the seat so that all controls and switches can be used.
- (d) Adjust (if necessary) the rear view mirrors.
- (e) Make sure all doors are properly shut.
- (f) Check the movement of the handbrake after applying the footbrake, then the movement of the footbrake after the handbrake has been applied. Should there be excessive movement in either brake, the vehicle should not be moved until the fault has been rectified.
- (g) Put the seat belt on, unless you are exempt from wearing one.
- (h) Make sure any passenger(s) in the rear have put their seatbelts on.

Above:
Moving Off
The driver must use the mirrors before moving off.

Numerous drivers get into a vehicle each day and take it for granted that the tyres, fluid levels and brakes are correct. Tyre pressures and all fluid levels should be checked at least once a week, the brakes daily.

When the starting routine has been completed, the engine can be started. After the engine has been started, look at the fuel gauge to make sure there is sufficient fuel in the tank.

Moving Off

Immediately after the correct gear has been selected, the driver must use the mirrors to check the movement and position of any approaching traffic from the rear that could make it unsafe to move off. All-round observation must then be taken so that the presence of any pedestrians is known. A signal of intention to move out should be considered — though, if given, it gives no protection or right of way whatsoever. If there is no potential danger, no signal is required. The driver should move off only when he is sure it is safe to do so, and not before; as a result the manoeuvre will not create

Right:
A driver has a restricted view to the rear when using the mirrors, therefore all-round observation must be taken by looking over the left and right shoulders before the decision to move off can be made.

potential danger or inconvenience to any other road user or pedestrian.

After moving off, you will in all probability have to slow down or stop in the near future. It must, therefore, be borne in mind that the correct operation of the brakes is of the utmost importance to the control of the vehicle. It is for this reason that the operation of the footbrake is checked as soon as possible after moving off, even though the movement of the brake pedal was checked while the vehicle was stationary. The driver must make sure that no traffic is following before a brake test is made.

The object of the test is to see how the vehicle responds to a normal application of the brakes when applied firmly. The vehicle should pull up on a straight course, without pulling to either side, and with equal braking to all wheels. While carrying out the brake test the operation of inertia seat belts can also be checked.

View from the Vehicle

It is the responsibility of the driver to have the best possible observation from the vehicle at all times. A driver sitting in the correct position at the steering wheel must cover the area to the front and sides through an arc of approximately 180°. This can only be achieved by ensuring that the windscreen and other windows are kept clean inside and out. Many vehicles can be seen with the windscreen and other windows cover in grime, and in consequence are opaque, causing the driver to peer through the filth in front of him. It is an offence to drive a motor vehicle that does not comply with the regulations concerning visual transmission of light and freedom from obstruction to vision. The windscreen and other windows must be kept clean. Stickers placed on the windscreen and other windows can obscure a driver's view, and therefore should not be placed there. In some vehicles, lucky charms and mascots can be seen hanging from the interior; these swing about in front of the driver, thereby causing distraction and obscuring the view of the road, which is potentially dangerous. The mirrors should be properly adjusted so that the best possible view to the rear is gained.

The driver should make sure the windscreen wipers and washers are in proper working order. Particles of dust and grit will at times collect on the windscreen, therefore the washers should be used to assist cleaning before the wipers are used, otherwise the windscreen could get scratched and wiper rubbers damaged.

Furthermore, the bodywork of the vehicle — ie roof supports, door pillars and other parts — can obstruct a driver's view and should be considered when adjusting the mirrors. Adverse weather conditions too can greatly reduce effective observation.

Adverse Weather

Allowances should always be made for mistakes of other road users. It is unsafe to assume that another driver will react correctly to any given situation; he may have passed his driving test only that day, or be driving a strange or defective vehicle. He may be a naturally aggressive or thoughtless driver, or attempting to drive beyond his capabilities for the prevailing conditions in order to keep an urgent appointment.

It is surprising — but true — that the average driver is not aware of one essential fact: he should always be in a position to stop his vehicle well within the distance he sees to be clear. Horrific pile-ups in mist, fog and smoke prove that this rule has not been applied. It has been said that concentration and road observation are very closely related, for without the former, success in the latter cannot possibly be achieved. The value and assessment of what is seen allows a driving plan to be formulated.

When fog is seen, the Advanced Driver will apply Feature Two of the System of Car Control (Mirrors, Signals and Speed). The headlights (with the beam dipped) and rear fog lamps should be switched on, and the mirrors are used to check the movement and position of following traffic. An arm signal ('I intend to slow down or stop') should be considered to inform following traffic of the intention to slow down. Speed is reduced by deceleration or proper application of the brakes, and a safe following distance maintained from the vehicle in front, thus giving the driver and other road users time and distance to pull up well within the distance that can be seen to be clear. It cannot be stressed too strongly that this procedure must be implemented in good time, and not when it is too late or not at all, which is often the case. Some drivers rely on warning lights to inform them of danger, instead of using their eyes to see the danger. It should be borne in mind that fog can form randomly at any place, quite possibly where warning lights are not sited.

When driving on stretches of road affected by heavy rain, a curtain of spray from other vehicles will reduce a driver's view of the road ahead. In such conditions the driver must use the headlamps with the beam dipped, thereby informing other road users of his presence. A driver, aware he is catching up with another vehicle, must decide either to adjust his speed and follow at a safe distance while it makes reasonable progress, or overtake at the first opportunity. If the decision to overtake is made, the mirrors must be used to check the movements of any following traffic, and he should consider the need for a signal before changing course.

It must be borne in mind that the road situation can change at any moment — for example, a high-sided vehicle could be affected by cross wind, or could pull out to overtake. On a two-lane motorway, heavy goods vehicles are permitted to use the overtaking lane, but are prohibited from using the third or fourth lane where such lanes exist.

The speed of the vehicle to be overtaken must be considered, as the higher speed required to overtake could induce 'aqua planing', particularly if the tread depth of the tyres is getting near the minimum legal limit. On a badly drained road surface at a speed in excess of 50mph, the driver's ability and the type, condition and limitations of the vehicle must all be considered before the decision to overtake can be made. If there is any doubt, the driver should not attempt to overtake.

Fatigue

Travelling at high speed requires total concentration and mental alertness, and driving a considerable distance without stopping (but within the law), possibly combined with night-time dazzle and ever-changing conditions of visibility, will result in tiredness. Good ventilation and driving with a window open can assist to delay the effects. However, when the driver feels his driving skills are deteriorating, he should pull up at a suitable place and freshen up. This can be achieved by washing his face, taking refreshment (hot drink and food) then going for a walk to improve his circulation. When he is refreshed, it should be safe for him to proceed with his journey.

If the driver is totally exhausted there is no option, in the interest of safety, but to park the vehicle, book in at a hotel and gain a good night's rest.

6 Defensive Driving

Defensive driving is part of Advanced Driving. For example, a driver who is looking well ahead and concentrating on his driving will recognise potentially dangerous situations in good time. Therefore, the driver has time to take the necessary action and to compensate for possible risks created by other road users. Each feature of the system of car control must be considered on the approach to any hazard, and the appropriate feature applied as necessary.

Too many people drive motor vehicles thinking of other matters instead of concentrating on their driving. In consequence, they fail to recognise potential danger and get involved in or cause an accident. For example, unless a large goods vehicle has been driven, it cannot be appreciated or understood by the majority of car drivers, why the driver of the goods vehicle has to position his vehicle so far from the kerb before turning left. The car driver thinks the driver of the large goods vehicle is in the wrong lane, in consequence positions his car on the nearside, and is most surprised when the car is about to be crushed by the trailer of the goods vehicle when it turns left.

Right:
The driver of the car can see the signal of intent given by the driver of the large goods vehicle, and has, therefore, held back and stopped in the correct position. This allows the goods vehicle to use the nearside lane when it turns left.

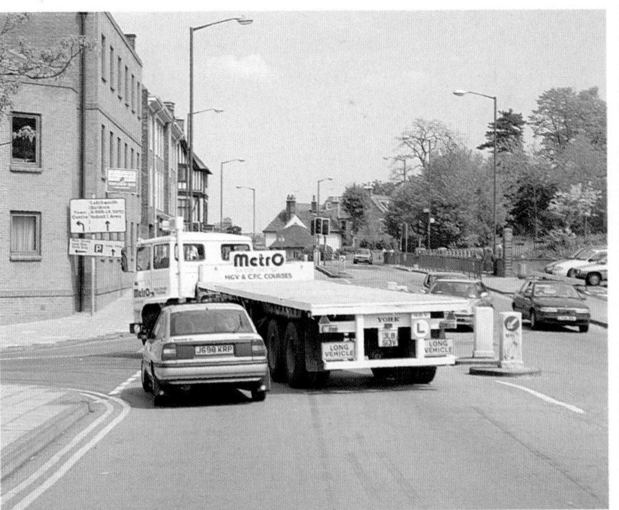

Far left:
The driver of the car is unaware of the amount of road a large goods vehicle requires to complete a left turn, and is, therefore, about to learn the expensive way, if the driver of the lorry has not checked the nearside mirror/s.

Left:
The driver of the car is trying to creep down the nearside of the lorry. This foolhardy manoeuvre will soon be realised by the driver of the car.

Bottom far left:
The driver of the car is trying to overtake the lorry on a roundabout. He has not appreciated the length of the vehicle and the amount of road needed.

Left:
The lorry is about to leave a roundabout. At the same time an impatient car driver is trying to overtake the lorry on the nearside which is irresponsible driving, and as seen is dangerous.

Right:

When approaching a mini-roundabout at the same time as a large vehicle is seen approaching from the right, whose intention is to turn left, you should pull up well before the Give Way lines, thereby giving the approaching driver all the available road that is needed to complete the left turn. Unlike the car driver illustrated here, who has forced the driver of the bus to stop. He was either thoughtless or not aware that a large vehicle needs a lot more room to complete the manoeuvre than a car.

Below right:

When travelling along a road that has parked vehicles on both sides, Feature Two of the System of car control should be applied. This means being able to stop, should an approaching vehicle come into the road too fast for the prevailing conditions.

Far right:

An inconsiderate driver has parked a vehicle on the approach to a roundabout. A vehicle can be seen approaching from the right, therefore when approaching this type of hazard, Feature Two of the System (mirrors, signal/s and speed) should be applied in anticipation of the vehicle approaching from the right, turning left.

Left:
These horse riders are not complying with the advice given in the *Highway Code*. When following horse riders as in this situation, there is no option but to remain behind them and wait for a clear view of the road ahead, before any decision to overtake/pass them can even be considered.

Bottom far left:
Prior to overtaking the vehicle in front the driver has held back until the cyclists have gone through, rather than pressing on. By pressing on the driver would have created a hazard and caused the cyclists to take evasive action.

Below left:
The traffic sign informs a driver that there is unmarked Cross Roads ahead. The view of the junction is obscured to either side, therefore the mirrors must be used and speed reduced (Feature Two) applied. In doing so the driver should approach the junction with extreme caution, and therefore be able to stop should the need arise.

Right:

By looking well ahead a pedestrian can be seen about to board a bus; at the same time oncoming traffic can also be seen. The defensive driver will use the mirrors, consider slowing down if necessary, thereby allowing time for the bus to move off.

Below right:

While driving at 70mph (which equals 103ft/sec and is the maximum speed limit for this dual carriageway) a car can be seen approaching the road from the exit of the garage. It must not be taken for granted that the driver will stop and look for approaching traffic. Even if the driver looks towards you he might not be able to see you, or may underestimate your speed and distance. Thus the mirrors should be used, enabling you to be aware of any following traffic.

Should the driver emerge into the road, and thus into your path, you have two options: reduce speed; or, if safe to do so, change course to the overtaking lane. The use of the horn could be considered, but would be of little use, once the driver has emerged into your path.

Far left:
While waiting to emerge from a side road, a driver should not accept a left turn direction indicator signal as proof of an approaching driver's true indintention. The waiting driver should look for supporting evidence — eg a considerable reduction of speed and a change of course — before the decision can be made to emerge into the junction.

Left:
If the driver waiting to emerge had taken the signal of the approaching car for granted, a collision would have occurred.

Below left:
What this car driver should have done was to signal his intention to stop when he was level with the vehicle waiting to emerge.

7 The System of Car Control

The System of Car Control, devised by Lord Cottenham for the Metropolitan Police Motor Driving School in 1937, is a system or drill, each feature of which is considered, in sequence, by the driver at the approach to any hazard. It is the basis upon which the whole technique of good driving is built, and still forms the basis for instruction for police drivers today.

A hazard is anything which contains an element of actual or potential danger. There are three types:

- (a) Physical features, such as a road junction, roundabout, bend or hill crest and dip (dead ground).
- (b) Those created by the position or movement of other road users.
- (c) Those created by variations in road surface or weather conditions.

By definition, every Feature of the System is considered on the approach to any hazard, only the Features of the System that are applicable to a given situation are used, but whichever features are used they must always be in the correct sequence. Only by constant practice and self-discipline, can the skill in the application of the System be acquired.

Features of the System

The Features of the System of Car Control are:

- **1: Course** — The driver, having seen the hazard, decides on the correct line on the approach. He looks in his mirrors and, if it is necessary to change position to obtain the correct course, a deviation signal is considered.
- **2: Mirrors, Signals and Speed** — The mirrors are used again and, if the intention is to turn right or left at the hazard, consideration must be given to use a signal of intent, as illustrated in the *Highway Code*. Any reduction in speed for the hazard will be accomplished at this stage, preceded by a slowing down signal if appropriate.
- **3: Gear** — After all unwanted speed has been lost, the correct gear is selected which should be the most responsive for the road speed of the vehicle.
- **4: Mirrors and Signals** — It is essential to look in the mirrors again and, if not previously given a signal of intent should be used, if it will assist another road user and/or pedestrian to be aware of your intention.
- **5: Horn** — Sound the horn, to give warning of your presence, if necessary. It should not be used as a means to force the right-of-way.
- **6: Acceleration** — The correct amount of acceleration (if safe to do so) is applied to leave the hazard safely.

It will be seen from the examples given that the System of Car Control is used on the approach to all hazards, although every Feature may not, in fact, need to be applied. Once the driver has learned the System he should practice it continually. He will find through experience that although circumstances may alter on the approach to a hazard, requiring a change in driving plan, the application of the System will become instinctive and form the basis upon which the finer points of driving can be built. Over the years many people have criticised Lord Cottenham's technique of driving, but no one has ever bettered his System of Car Control. The opinions and differences on driving a motor vehicle are many, but how many self-opinionated drivers can prove they are the perfect driver? None.

The System for a Left Turn at Crossroads

The national speed limit of 60mph applies to this road. Therefore in built-up areas, the System is more closely formulated than on a road which has a 60mph or greater speed limit for cars.

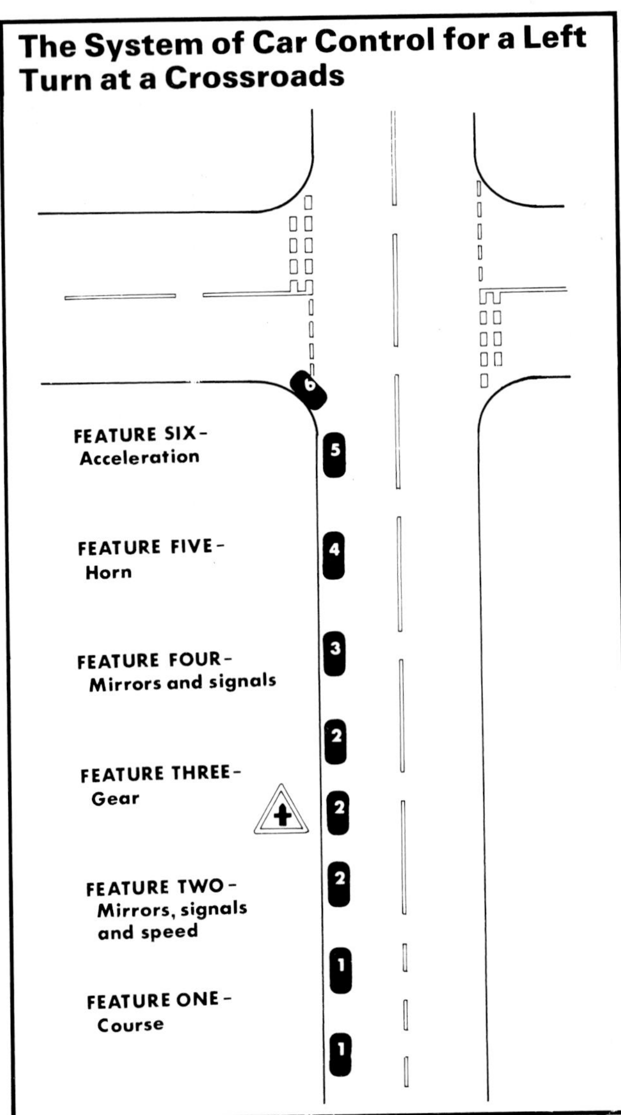

Left:

Feature One: Course

Course: **The driver is on the ideal course being well to the left of the road, requiring little or no deviation, as the road ahead can be seen to be clear. The mirrors must be used.**

Below left:

Feature Two: Mirrors, Signal and Speed

Mirrors: **The mirrors must be used to check the movements and position of any following traffic.**

Right:
Signal: **If any traffic is following, and/or waiting to emerge from the junction, a Direction Indicator Signal of intent to turn left should be given.**

Far right:
Speed: **In all probability it will be necessary to reduce speed. This should be achieved by braking, except for slight variation in speed, when deceleration will be sufficient.**

Below right:

Feature Three: Gear

Gear: **When all unwanted road speed has been lost, a gear should be selected to match that of the road speed. A lower gear is also more responsive to slight movement on the accelerator. The driver should look to his right and left, to gain that brief but valuable information of any traffic that could be approaching the junction.**

Far left:

Feature Four: Mirrors and Signal

Mirrors and Signal: **Immediately after the gear change the mirrors should be used again, as there could be traffic following that was not previously visible. The driver (if practically possible) should look into the road on the left, to make sure it is still safe to turn left. If a left turn signal has not been given yet, it should now be considered, more so if following traffic can be seen in the mirrors. Approaching traffic intending to turn right, and if any pedestrian(s) are waiting to or about to cross the road that is about to be joined. Give way to pedestrians already crossing when you turn. They have priority.**

Above left:

Feature Five: Horn

Horn: **The circumstances dictate the use of the horn. A driver should give way to pedestrians who are crossing the road.**

Left:

Feature Six: Acceleration

Acceleration: **The correct degree of acceleration to leave the hazard will be determined by the condition of the road surface, and the presence of any potential danger.**

Right:

Turning Left or Right from a Narrow Road

An Advanced Driver, looking well ahead, will apply the System in good time. His vision to the right and left is obstructed by a tall hedge and a wall of a barn. The road is narrow, allowing one lane of traffic in each direction, and for that reason the position of the vehicle should be well to the left. The adopted position would be the same for a right turn, because of the reasons stated.

Below right:

The vehicle is less than half its length from the Give Way line. No vision into the road to be joined is available to either side, thus the decision to stop has been made. By doing so, additional time has been made available for the driver to check the junction properly before deciding whether to emerge. If in doubt, WAIT.

Far left:

Turning Left into a Narrow Road

The driver is going to turn left into a narrow road. The view to the left is totally obscured by the presence of a tall hedge, therefore no information is available to the driver as to what potential danger could be round the corner. Features One to Four have been implemented and, therefore, all unwanted speed has been lost with the correct gear engaged. Feature Five (The Horn) could be used, but gives you no right of way. Should a vehicle appear from the left there is no option but to stop, thereby allowing the driver to emerge into the junction before you can complete your turn.

Above left:

The driver is on the apex of the turn. When the left turn has been completed, and if safe to do so, she can apply Feature Six (acceleration).

Left:

The driver has positioned the vehicle in a lane designated for traffic turning left.

The System for a Right Turn

A right turn at cross roads is one of the most difficult and potentially dangerous manoeuvres, because other road users may be entering the junction from other directions at the same time. It is therefore of the utmost importance for your own safety and that of other road users, that the application of the Six Features of the System must be considered on the approach to the hazard, either in full or those Features applicable to particular circumstances at the time. It should always be borne in mind that the situation at the time dictates what Feature(s) should be used, as what can be seen to be clear in one second could change in another. Whichever Features are used, they should always be in the correct sequence.

Right:

Feature One: Course

***Course:* If travelling in the nearside, it will be necessary to move out to the ideal course to just left of the centre of the road, or into a lane designated for right turn traffic. This should be done in good time, having regard to any road markings, volume of traffic, your speed and that of other vehicles on the approach to the junction.**

Top right:

***Course:* The mirrors must be used, thereby being aware of the speed and position of any following traffic. An 'I intend to move out' direction indicator signal should be given if any traffic is following.**

Far right:

***Course:* When safe to do so, move out to the correct position for a right turn.**

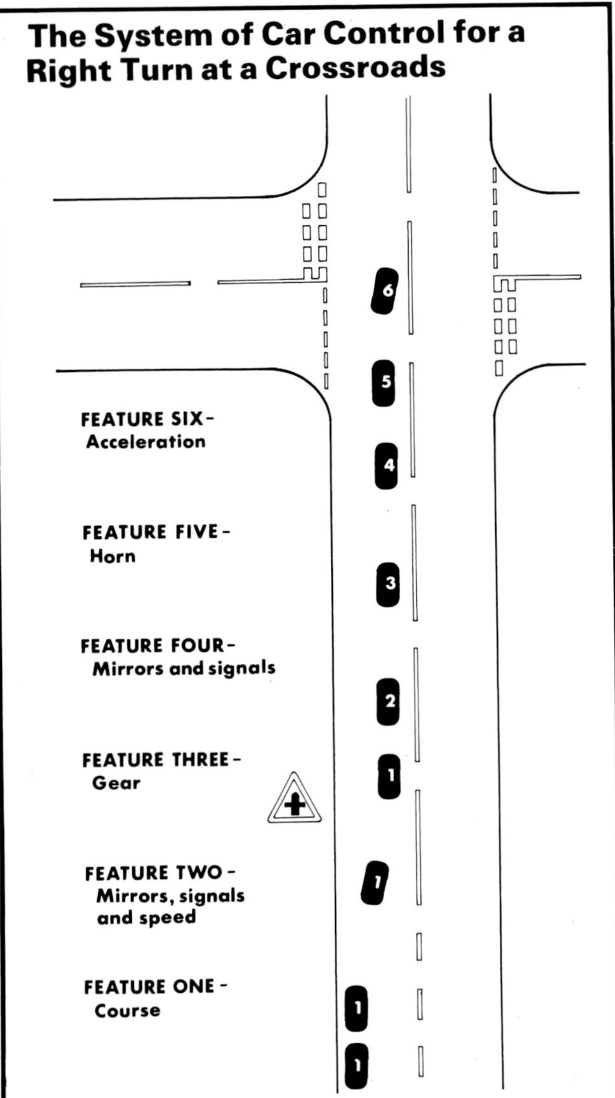

Left:
***Course*: The correct position for a right turn is just left of the centre line road markings**

Below left:

Feature Two: Mirrors, Signal and Speed

***Mirrors*: The mirrors must be used to assess the speed and position of any vehicles behind.**

***Signal:* The need for an 'I intend to turn right' direction indicator signal should now be considered unless it was used to change course and is, therefore, still operating.**

Right:
Speed: **In all probability it will be necessary to reduce speed; any reduction of speed should be achieved by braking, unless only a slight variation in speed is required, in which case deceleration will be sufficient.**

Below right:

Feature Three: Gear

Gear: **When the speed of the vehicle has been reduced, a gear should be selected to match the road speed of the vehicle. The gear selected should be able to respond readily to slight accelerator pressure. A vehicle fitted with automatic transmission will select an appropriate gear to match that of the road speed of the vehicle, when the unnecessary road speed has been reduced.**

Left:

Feature Four: Mirrors, and Signals

Mirrors: **When the gear has been selected, the mirrors should be used again, as the movement of any following traffic previously seen could have been changed.**

Signals: **If a direction indicator signal has not been required till now, it should be considered. If a right turn signal is being used, the use of an 'I intend to turn right' arm signal should now be considered, to confirm your intention to change course. This applies particularly if the sun is behind you. The driver should look to the right and left to gain that brief but valuable information of any traffic that could be approaching the junction, or pedestrian about to cross the road.**

Below left:

Feature Five: Horn

Horn: **There can be occasions when all reasonable safety precautions have been taken by the driver, but it will still be necessary to draw the attention of another road user or pedestrian, who is obviously vulnerable, to your presence. Therefore, an audible warning should be considered, so that the other road user is aware of your approach. It must be borne in mind that the other road user or pedestrian may have a hearing defect or may be listening to a radio, thus you should take nothing for granted. If something can be seen that can prevent you entering the road you intend to join, eg pedestrians who are crossing the road, the mirrors should be used and you should stop and wait until you can complete the turn safely.**

Right:

Feature Six: Acceleration

Acceleration: **When you are sure it is safe to proceed, and the condition of the road surface has been assessed, a small amount of acceleration should be used to take you round the apex of the turn. In doing so you will maintain stability of the vehicle while turning. When the vehicle is on a straight course, and the road ahead can be seen to be clear, normal acçeleration to leave the hazard can be applied.**

Below right:

On some roads there is a lane designated for traffic turning right. This lane has white diagonal hatch markings or chevrons which lead to a broken or continuous white line. Their purpose is to separate through traffic from vehicles turning right. The driver illustrated is in the correct position for turning right.

Far left:

Another example of protecting traffic turning right is on a dual carriageway that has a 70mph speed limit is illustrated here. An approach lane has been provided, which allows traffic turning right to move out of the overtaking lane. This reduces the possibility of rear-end collisions, between through traffic and vehicles waiting to turn.

Above left:

When following a vehicle on a dual carriageway which, to all intents, appears to be overtaking, you should never assume the true intention of the driver in front, as this could lead to numerous problems.

Left:

Because you did not know what the true intention of the driver in front was, what appeared to be an 'I intend to move out' direction indicator signal was, in fact an, 'I intend to turn right' signal. The driver is now reducing speed to turn right. As stated, never assume; make sure before you act, otherwise you could be set up, or set yourself up, for an accident.

Below:
This aerial view of a large gyratory roundabout shows a two-way traffic system. This allows double the volume of traffic to use the roundabout. The 'Give Way' rule, to traffic on the right, applies.

Right:
This roundabout in Berkshire has a road going through its centre, which assists the movement of traffic. The movement of traffic going round and through the roundabout is controlled by traffic light signals.

Bottom right:
The configuration of mini-roundabouts may seem confusing at first sight. The appropriate features of the System should be applied as necessary on the approach to each hazard.

Roundabouts

In 1990 there were estimated 113,000 accidents at or on a roundabout. It is, therefore, evident that 113,000 road users involved in the accidents did not comply with the advice given in the *Illustrated Highway Code*. Roundabouts are designed to assist traffic flow at junctions, by allowing traffic to enter and leave by different roads, with the minimum of inconvenience or danger. Roundabouts vary in size and shape from the large gyratory complexes which can have a two-way traffic system, to a mini or conventional size roundabout which are one-way systems in which traffic circulates in a clockwise direction. When approaching a roundabout, the driver should look to the right as soon as practicably possible, in doing so he should be able to see and assess the speed and position of approaching vehicles. There will be times when this will not be possible, either due to temporary obstructions or a speed reducing measure that has been placed. Speed reducing measures are designed to encourage drivers to reduce speed on the approach to the roundabout.

The general rule is to give way to traffic from the immediate right, unless road markings indicate otherwise, but keep moving if the way is clear. The System of Car Control should be applied on the approach to the roundabout, thus allowing time to react to faults that can be committed by other road users. The 'Give Way' rule at roundabouts was introduced in 1964.

Far left:
Like any other roundabout, vehicle positioning is of the utmost importance. A driver should go round the white 'blob', and not over it. It should be borne in mind that very long vehicles may find difficulty in conforming to this rule.

Bottom left:
Some drivers have no regard to the direction arrows painted on the road. This driver is going round the roundabout the wrong way, and is therefore committing an offence.

Left:
This lamp post, erected on an island on a mini-roundabout, encourages drivers to adopt a correct course and reduce speed.

Right:
There could be a mini-roundabout that has been put in the wrong place like this one, thereby giving road users no choice but to go over it.

The six features of the System of Car Control must be considered for all hazards. Should the situation change on the approach, you may have to make a complete re-assessment, starting again from Feature One. The following examples show the features of the system being applied in sequence, as the road ahead can be seen to be clear.

Top far right:

The System: Left Turn at a Roundabout
Feature One: Course

Course: **The driver, having seen the hazard, should be on the ideal course well to the left of the road; but bear in mind circumstances could change before you reach the hazard.**

Right:

Feature Two: Mirrors, Signal and Speed

Mirrors: **The mirrors must be used so that the position of any following traffic will be known.**

Far right:
Signal: **If traffic was seen in the mirrors, an 'I intend to turn left' direction indicator signal should be used, otherwise its use should be considered.**

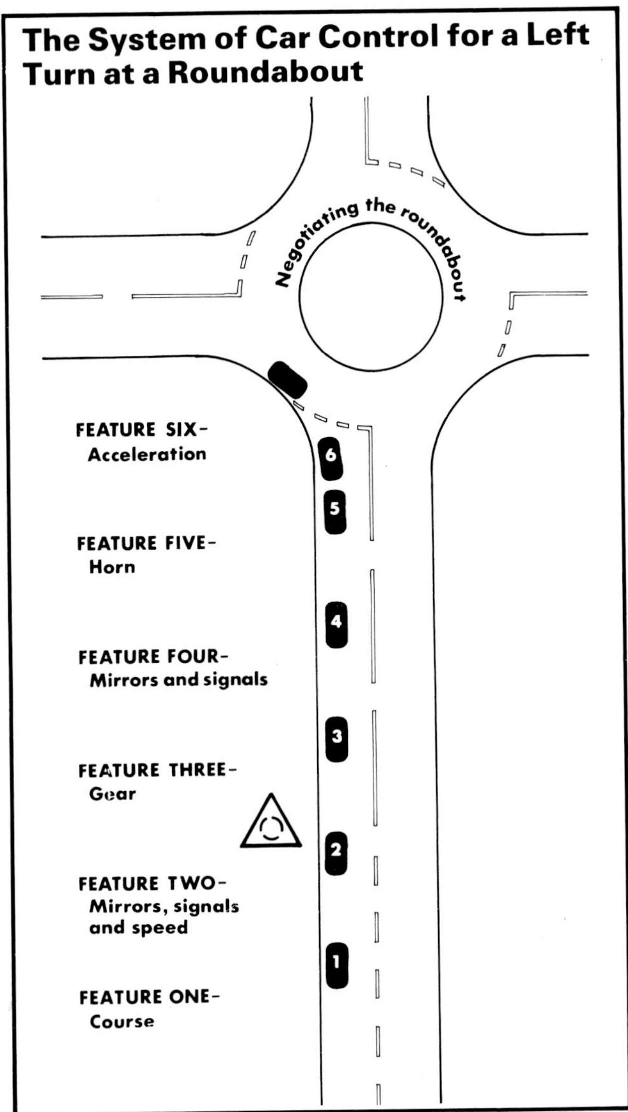

Left:
Speed: **All unwanted road speed is being lost by braking, except for a minor variation in speed when deceleration will be sufficient. It must be borne in mind that the speed on the approach is related to the view into the roads to the right and left. The less view the driver has into these roads the slower the speed and, therefore, he will be able to give way to any traffic approaching from the right.**

Below left:

Feature Three: Gear

Gear: **When all unwanted road speed has been lost, a gear that will be most responsive to the accelerator for the road speed of the vehicle should be selected.**

Right:

Feature Four: Mirrors and Signal

Mirrors and Signal: **Immediately after the gear change the driver should use the mirrors to check the situation behind, as there could be traffic following that was not previously visible. If there is traffic catching up, an 'I intend to turn left' direction indicator signal should be considered, if not previously given at Feature Two. The nearside exterior mirror should now be used.**

Far right:

Feature Five: Horn

Horn: **The horn should be considered if it will assist to warn another road user or pedestrian(s) of your presence. The driver should give way to any pedestrian(s) who are crossing the road that is about to be joined, in which case the horn should not be used to harass them.**

Right:

Feature Six: Acceleration

Acceleration: **When the driver is sure it is safe to join the roundabout, gentle acceleration should be used, until any potential dangers have been passed, then firm acceleration can be applied to leave the hazard, providing the road ahead can be seen to be clear.**

Far left:

The System: Straight Ahead at a Roundabout

Feature One: Course

Course: **The position of the vehicle on the approach to the roundabout should be on the nearside, unless conditions or road markings dictate otherwise. It should be borne in mind there could be two lanes on the approach to the roundabout, but only one lane leaving it.**

Left:

Feature Two: Mirrors, Signals and Speed

Mirrors: **The mirrors must be used, so that the presence and position of any following traffic is known.**

Bottom far left:

Signals and Speed: **If traffic was seen in the mirrors an 'I intend to slow down' arm signal should be considered or a 'Stop Light Signal' should be used, so that other drivers are aware of your intention. All unwanted speed should be lost in good time having due regard to the necessity to give way to traffic from the immediate right.**

Left:

Feature Three: Gear

Gear: **When all unwanted speed has been lost, a gear that will be most responsive to the accelerator for the road speed of the vehicle should be selected.**

Right:

Feature Four: Mirrors and Signals

Mirrors and Signals: **Immediately after the gear change the mirrors should be used again, so that you will be aware of any following traffic. As your intention is to follow the road ahead, a deviation signal would not be required.**

Far right:

Feature Five: Horn

Horn: **Unless an unusual circumstance should arise, the use of the horn would not normally be necessary.**

Below right:

Feature Six: Acceleration

Acceleration: **The amount of acceleration that can be applied will depend on the prevailing circumstances — the condition of the road surface and eg, other potential hazards which are likely to develop. The chosen lane should be maintained through the roundabout.**

Far right:

Signal: **An 'I intend to turn left' direction indicator signal should be used if it will inform another road user of your intention. A signal to leave the roundabout should be given as you pass the exit immediately before the junction you intend to leave. The nearside mirror should be used.**

Far left:
Acceleration: **If it is safe to do, accelerate away from the hazard. if an indicator signal was used, make sure it is cancelled.**

Left:

The System: Right Turn at a Roundabout Feature One: Course

Course: **If travelling on the nearside when the hazard is seen, it will be necessary to move out to an ideal course just left of the centre of the road. It should be borne in mind there could be more than one lane on the approach to the roundabout, therefore a change of course should be made in good time. The mirrors must be used so that the position of any following traffic is known. If traffic is seen in the mirrors, an 'I intend to move out' signal should be given.**

Far left:
When safe to do so, change course to just left of the centre of the road.

Left:
The driver is on the correct course for a right turn.

Right:

Feature Two: Mirrors, Signals and Speed

Mirrors: **The mirrors must be used again, so that you will be aware of the position of any following traffic or change in circumstances.**

Below right:

Signals: **If traffic was seen in the mirrors a signal of intent should be given.**

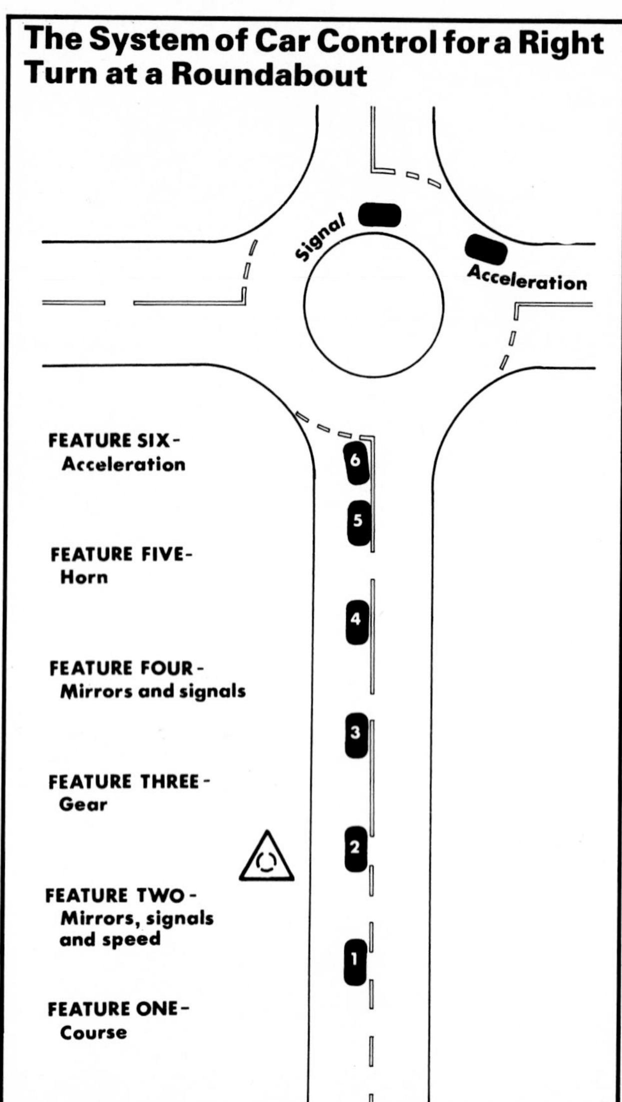

Far left:

Speed: **All unwanted speed should be lost by proper use of the brakes or deceleration, bearing in mind the following driver maybe following too closely. The speed on the approach is closely related to what can and cannot be seen to be clear.**

Left:

Feature Three: Gear

Gear: **When all unwanted road speed has been lost, a gear that will be most responsive to the accelerator for the road speed of vehicle should be selected.**

Bottom far left:

Feature Four: Mirrors and Signal

Mirrors and Signal: **The mirrors must be used again, because the situation behind may have changed since Feature Two. If a signal has not been used, it should now be considered.**

Left:

Feature Five: Horn

Horn: **If a situation develops requiring the use of the horn, it should be used.**

Right:

Feature Six: Acceleration

***Acceleration:* The presence of any other vehicles ahead will dictate how much acceleration can be applied. The present position on the roundabout should be maintained, unless road markings or traffic signs dictate otherwise.**

Far right:

A signal to leave the roundabout should be given as you pass the exit immediately before the junction you intend to leave. The nearside mirror should be used and a glance over the left shoulder will do much to assist your awareness of the presence of any other traffic on your nearside.

Below right:

Any increase of speed may still be undesirable until the conditions allow otherwise.

Cornering and Bends

There have been numerous fatal accidents on bends that should never have occurred, but have for a number of reasons. The biggest contributory factor to these accidents was excessive speed at the wrong time and wrong place. Some drivers approached a bend giving no thought to or appreciation of its severity or length and, in consequence, approached at a speed far too high for the prevailing conditions. They were, therefore, outside the bounds of safety.

The conditions of the road surface, camber or crossfall of the road, the condition of the vehicle, and its load was not considered either. There are warning signs on the approach to most bends, that warn a driver of the type of bend(s) ahead, which could be a single, double or series of bends. However, it should always be borne in mind that some roads have no warning signs or road markings on the approach to or on a bend. It should, therefore, not be assumed that there will be any warning. There are also the physical features of a bend that some drivers are not aware of or fail to recognise.

Cornering is a term to describe the driving of a motor vehicle around a corner or bend. It is an important part of the skills of driving for a driver to have a thorough understanding of the principles involved before a safe technique can be mastered. This is a contributory factor that assists an advanced driver to be a safer driver, compared with another driver who has not received any professional driving instruction since passing the 'L' test. The following examples show the type of bends, vision and condition of the road surface that a driver must recognise on the approach to a bend, and apply the appropriate features of the System, thereby formulating a safe driving plan on the approach to the hazard. Thus the driver will be in the correct position on the road travelling at the right speed for the given situation, with the correct gear engaged. In doing so he will be able to stop within the distance that can be seen to be clear.

Principles

- (A) The driver must be concentrating and planning well ahead, and be able to recognise the type and severity of the bend, and be aware of other potential danger(s) such as a concealed entrance and pedestrians walking in the road. Therefore the driver should be in the correct position on the road, on the approach to the hazard.
- (B) The vehicle should be travelling at the correct speed for what can be seen, and the type of bend.
- (C) The correct gear, which can respond best to the accelerator, should be selected.

Left:
On the approach to this bend, a warning sign, combined with road markings, assists a driver to recognise the severity of the bend before it is reached.

Below:
There are no warning signs or road markings to inform a driver of the severity of the bend on the approach to, or on, this bend. What can be seen is a smooth road surface, an adverse camber and a sharp bend. The wall, on the right, completely obscures a driver's view across the bend, thus no advanced observation as to the severity of the bend or any other potential danger can be seen from this position.

Right:
On this bend, a driver will be able to gain advanced observation of the road ahead by looking through the railings.

Far right:
A driver approaching this bend has additional information as to the type of bend. Apart from the road markings, telegraph poles can also indicate the severity of a bend.

Below right:
At certain times of the year, crops grown in the fields will give a driver advanced advanced information to the severity of a bend(s).

Bottom far right:
By looking across this bend, a large goods vehicle can be seen. This will give a clue to the length of the bend.

Far left:
The traffic sign warns a driver of potential danger at the end of the bend that cannot be seen on the approach. Consequently speed should be reduced so that the vehicle can be stopped within the distance that can be seen to be clear.

Left:
A car driver, approaching this acute left-hand bend, will gain no advanced information of any approaching traffic. Thus the appropriate features of the System should be applied. Feature Five (horn) of the System should be used to warn any approaching road user not in view of your presence.

Bottom far left:
On the approach to this acute right-hand bend no advance information of approaching traffic can be gained, not even by looking through the gap in the wall. Only the severity of the bend can be seen.

Left:
The driver is keeping well to the left (course) and applying Features Two to Five.

Above:
The driver is keeping well to the left on the apex of the bend, thereby making an allowance for mistakes that could be made by an approaching driver.

Above right:
A farm entrance can be seen on the approach to this sharp right-hand bend. Mud can be seen all over the road; this, combined with the possibility of what could emerge from the farm and approaching traffic that cannot be seen, should give a driver approaching this situation adequate advance warning that Features One to Three of the System should have been applied.

- (D) When the correct speed and gear have been selected for the bend, the vehicle should (if safe to do so) be driven at a constant speed with the engine just pulling, until the road ahead can be seen to be clear, when the accelerator can be used to the driver's advantage.

Safety Factors

By applying these principles, the following safety factors will be achieved as the vehicle is about to leave the bend or corner.

- (A) The vehicle will be in the correct position on and side of the road.
- (B) Because the vehicle is travelling at the correct speed for the hazard, it will be able to remain there.
- (C) The driver will be able to stop within the distance that can be seen to be clear.

Vehicle Roadworthiness

It is the driver's responsibility to make sure the vehicle to be driven is in good working order, and thereby complies with the Law. Tyre pressures should be kept to those recommended by the manufacturer. Any load including passengers should be evenly distributed otherwise the driver could experience an adverse affect on the behaviour of the vehicle while negotiating a corner or bend.

The Vehicle

The handling qualities and characteristics of vehicles can vary considerably between one vehicle and another. For example, one vehicle may be inclined to 'understeer' — responding less to the amount of steering being used — compared to another vehicle that may 'oversteer' and respond more to the use of the steering wheel. This is particularly noticeable if the vehicle has power-assisted steering. It is therefore important for a driver to be aware of the characteristics of the vehicle being driven. This, combined with a sound knowledge of the principles of cornering, will assist a driver to negotiate a corner/bend safely, with the minimum loss of stability, and with maximum safety.

Cornering Forces

A vehicle is most stable when travelling on a straight and even course, at a constant speed. However, when it is driven round a curve at speed, adverse forces are created that affect the road holding capabilities of a vehicle. If the tyres cannot retain sufficient grip on the road, the driver will be unable to maintain the selected course, therefore loss of stability or vehicle control will occur. As a result the driver, passenger(s) and any other road user(s) will be at the mercy of the elements.

To counteract the adverse force(s) of a vehicle when going round a bend at speed, some roads have a slope/camber, thereby

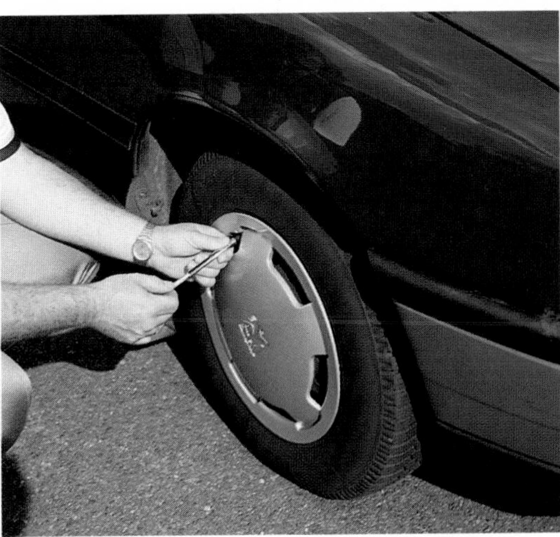

Far left:
The warning sign can be clearly seen. Apart from the information given, the potential danger(s) should be obvious and, therefore, speed should have been reduced and the driver must be prepared to stop if necessary.

Left:
It is the driver's responsibility to check that the condition and pressures of the tyres comply with the Law. While checking the pressures, make sure there is at least 1.6mm of tread depth across the breadth and around the entire circumference. The walls of the tyres must be free from cuts and bulges.

Bottom far left:
The camber on this bend will help to counteract the adverse forces. This will assist a driver to maintain control of the vehicle.

Left:
This is an example of 'tram lining' round a left-hand bend. The car is travelling at 60mph which equals 88ft/sec, which is the speed limit on this road. The driver has placed his vehicle in what he thought to be a safe position. The problem being, should the driver suddenly see a stationary vehicle, he will need 240ft to be able to stop on a dry road surface, but when wet, hard braking on the apex of a bend can be hazardous. The following pictures takes you through a series of bends using the System of Car Control.

reducing the outward force created by the speed being travelled. For example, when a vehicle is driven round a sharp left-hand bend, the weight of the vehicle is transferred to the offside front wheel. The faster the vehicle is travelling the greater the stress that will be applied on to the offside front wheel. At the same time, the nearside rear wheel may lift and lose contact with the road, this is exacerbated if the vehicle has firm suspension and if no passenger(s) or load is being carried. This stress factor also applies to the nearside front wheel when going round a sharp right-hand bend, this time the rear offside wheel may lift off the road. Therefore it should be borne in mind, the slower the speed being travelled the less stress will be put on to the front suspension and tyres.

One aspect of driving that has been discussed on numerous occasions over the years is, 'what is the safest procedure and road position a driver should adopt when approaching, on, and leaving a bend?'. Every day, drivers can be seen approaching a sharp bend too fast and too close to each other, allowing no margin of safety at all. On occasions the driver's view on the approach to and in the bend is very limited, but his speed is not. Speed has not been checked, because the vehicle(s) in front is moving at the same speed; the irresponsible assumption made by these drivers is that everything ahead must be clear. Another factor that has not been considered, is the speed limit in force at the time, of which the driver is unaware or has ignored, thereby making the irresponsible actions being taken more serious and thus potentially more dangerous.

One authority on driving recommends that a driver should 'tram line' round a bend (keeping the same distance from the kerb throughout the bend). This is good advice providing the vehicle is driven at a speed that can be stopped within the distance that can be seen to be clear. Accident reports show that in numerous accidents speed has been too fast and separation distance too close, thus not allowing for the necessary stopping distance for the speed being travelled.

The System of Car Control for Bends

As previously seen, occasions will arise when it will be impossible to obtain any advance information as to the severity or length of a bend. It is therefore of the utmost importance that when approaching a bend, a driver should, if and when practically possible, position his vehicle to obtain the best view around the bend (**Feature One Course**). In doing so, this will provide a greater margin of safety, maintain the maximum stability of the vehicle, and the driver will be able therefore to stop within the distance that can be seen to be clear. Respect for the *Highway Code* the law and the safety of other road users is part of Advanced Driving.

Below right:

Right-Hand Bend

Feature One: Course

Course: **Any advance information regarding the severity and length of the bend must be looked for, and road surfaces considered. The speed limit on this road is 60mph, and the car is travelling at 60mph. The ideal course is well to the left requiring little change from a normal driving position, thereby obtaining a better view into the bend ahead.**

Feature Two: Speed

Speed: **The mirrors must be used, so you will be aware of the presence and position of any following traffic. Any unwanted speed should now be lost, for the reasons already mentioned in this chapter.**

Feature Three: Gear

Gear: **The ideal gear should now be selected, to match that of the road speed, so that the engine is just pulling, and at the same time will be able to respond to the accelerator.**

Left:

Feature Four: Mirrors and Signal

Mirrors: **The mirrors must be used again, to make sure the situation behind has not changed. A signal would not be required. The use of the horn would not normally be used. As the view of the bend opens up as the driver reaches the apex of the bend, a slight change in course will be made.**

Below left:

Feature Six: Acceleration

Acceleration: **The driver is completing a slight change in course to just left of the centre road marking, in doing so will limit the cornering forces on the vehicle to a minimum by taking the shortest route across the bend. The accelerator is used so that the engine is just pulling. There could be a situation when it would be undesirable to use the accelerator at all. For example, when descending a hill, the presence of another road user, a pedestrian, or oil that has been spilt on the road.**

A left-hand bend can be seen ahead, no approaching traffic can be seen, therefore the decision to maintain the present course and speed is made.

Right:

Left-Hand Bend
Feature One: Course
Feature Two: Speed
Feature Three: Gear

Course: **On the approach to a left-hand bend, advance information can often be gained by positioning the vehicle just left of the centre road marking; in doing so a driver will obtain an earlier view as shown.**
Speed: **The mirrors should now be used and the present road speed assessed.**
Gear: **Should the road speed need to be reduced, a lower gear might have to be selected at this stage.**

Below right:

Feature Four: Mirror and Signal
Feature Five: Horn

Mirrors and Signals: **As the driver approaches the apex of the bend the view of the road ahead opens up. The mirrors should be used again. A signal would not be required nor the use of the horn.**

Far left:

Feature Six: Acceleration

Acceleration: **The driver is making a slight change in course to the nearside as the apex of the bend is reached. This will reduce the cornering forces on the vehicle to a minimum, at the same time an improved view of the road ahead will be obtained. The use of the accelerator has not changed since leaving the last bend. A warning sign can be seen and its message given is clear to see. Therefore no increase in road speed will be made.**

Above left:

The driver is maintaining his position on the nearside so that a good view of the road ahead can be gained. He has been warned that crossroads are ahead. Consequently each Feature of the System should be considered on the approach.

Left:

A traffic sign can be seen ahead and a gap in the hedge indicates the location of the junction. At this stage the mirrors should be used and each feature of the System should be considered on the approach to the hazard.

Right:

Because the view to either side of the junction is obscured, the mirrors were used and a change in course made to a safe position on the road for the prevailing conditions.

Below right:

Faults on Bends

Any reduction in speed must be achieved before reaching the hazard, and not like this driver who is braking hard and late as he enters the bend. It should also be remembered that when the footbrake is used, the stop lights signal thus informs any following road user that you are reducing speed. This is one reason why selecting a lower gear to reduce speed and then using the footbrake could be potentially dangerous.

8 Speed and Safety

Since the development of the motor car, the quest for speed has been desired by many. The motor car of today provides the speed so desired by drivers of earlier years. The additional power available today has been abused by many, and used at the wrong time and place. As a result speed has been the cause of many accidents, causing pain, grief and suffering. It is common knowledge that some drivers, knowing that their eyesight does not meet the standard required by law use all type of roads. In doing so, they commit an offence each time they drive. It is the responsibility of each and every driver to make sure he/she can see well beyond the minimum distance required in law. A person who is taking the 'L' driving test has to read a number plate of a vehicle from 20.5m (about 67ft); even if achieved with difficulty the test is still conducted. Should the person pass the test and then drive on a motorway at 70mph, the overall shortest stopping distance would be 96m (315ft); the lethal aspect of this fact should now be seen. Speed must also be related to a driver's concentration, ability, experience, the type, condition and limitation of the vehicle, the statutory speed restriction in force at the time, and the prevailing weather, road and traffic conditions. It should always be borne in mind, that the considered safe speed at the time for a given situation can change from one second to another, which some drivers do not consider or allow for. Therefore speed must be adjusted to suit the situation at the time and place. Speed is a relative factor and looked upon as something dangerous in itself, it is not; but if abused, it can be a killer — kill your speed not a pedestrian or other road user. This should be borne in mind every time you drive, the onus is always on the driver.

Far left:
To make sure drivers are aware that there is a 30mph statutory speed limit ahead 'count-down' markers on a sign have been placed at 300, 200 and 100yd intervals from the mandatory sign, thereby allowing drivers adequate time and distance to reduce speed.

Left:
There is a statutory speed limit of 20mph on this road. This, combined with speed humps, makes an additional contribution towards the safety of pedestrians.

Right:

This is another example of a speed-reducing measure. Width restrictions and speed humps assist to enforce the speed limit.

Top far right:

White line road markings have been employed as a 'traffic calming' measure, thereby reducing the driver's ability to overtake. At the same time, the measures assist residents adjacent to the road to gain a better view of approaching traffic.

Right:

Although this Class 'A' road has a speed limit of 30mph, problems with enforcement and a number of serious accidents meant that radical action was required. A Speed Detection camera has now been installed. If a driver goes past the camera at more than 30mph, the camera will take a picture of the vehicle committing the offence. The summons for speeding — showing date, time, place and speed — will be sent to the driver. Excessive speed can prove to be very expensive — it's not worth it.

9 Dead Ground

There are two types of 'dead ground', both of which hide potential danger:

- (1) That caused by a road having a steep dip, whereby approaching vehicle will not be seen until they near the summit.
- (2) That caused by a hump-back bridge, where oncoming vehicles will not be seen until reaching the crest.

The advanced driver will take into account what can and cannot be seen, and will therefore approach the hazard at a speed at which he can stop within the distance that can be seen to be clear. By doing so will prevent himself from becoming involved in an accident in the hidden stretch of road.

Above left:
The traffic sign combined with the view of the road ahead warns a driver of the potential danger.

Far left:
By looking well ahead a steep dip can be seen.

Left:
The traffic sign gives a clear warning that stationary traffic could be just beyond the bend. The mirrors should be used and speed reduced.

Right:
Traffic approaching from the other side of the hump-back bridge cannot be seen. At the same time your position on the road is not visible to an oncoming driver.

Below right:
The traffic sign gives a clear message: you should, therefore, act on the advice given.

10 Road Signs and Signals

To be of use, a traffic sign must give its message clearly and in good time for a road user to see it, understand its message and have time to act on the information given well before the hazard is reached. This is why symbols are used on traffic signs in the UK and throughout Europe; the message they give should be easily recognised. Traffic signs and road markings, combined with signals given by other road users, are the language of the road. Contrary to popular belief, some road users do not always see or fully understand the majority of road signs provided for his/her guidance. Thus if a sign is missed or not understood, an accident could occur. An advanced driver looking well ahead will recognise and understand the message given by a traffic sign. In doing so the driver will allow himself time to assess the situation and formulate a safe driving plan. The majority of traffic signs can be seen in the *Highway Code*.

In 1992 Continental traffic signs were used in Manchester for a new generation of trams, their official title being 'Light Rapid Transport System'. These new trams not only run on tracks on the road, but extend their use to using railway lines, thereby having a dual purpose, being a tram and train. Some of the traffic signs appertaining to trams are:

Below left:
The STOP sign is self-explanatory and must be complied with, regardless whether the road to either side can be seen to be clear. Also seen is a sign informing road users that the road to be crossed is a tram route. A 'Box' junction can also be seen.

Below:
If the STOP sign is not complied with when a tram is approaching, a fatal accident could occur.

Right:

This junction is controlled by traffic lights. These are showing a red signal. A 'box' junction can also be seen that has traffic queuing on the far side. When the green light signal is shown, and if traffic is still queuing as seen, a driver should not move forward unless the box junction can be cleared, otherwise a dangerous situation could occur.

Below right:

The reason for double white lines is clearly shown on the sign. They must be complied with.

Far left:

Traffic Signs

The safety of pedestrians and disabled people is of paramount importance, therefore the appropriate features of the System must be used, thereby reducing the possibility of potential danger.

Left:

The same advice applies to disabled drivers.

Bottom far left:

On seeing the sign, the mirrors must be used and preparation made to reduce speed or stop.

Below left:

English and Welsh languages are used on this traffic sign in Wales.

Right:
The message given by the traffic sign is clear. By looking well ahead the potential danger can be seen.

Far right:
An oncoming large goods vehicle — which the motorist will not see in advance — will in all probability need most of the road to negotiate the bend safely. The present situation that looks to be clear could change at any time.

Below right:
This unposed situation confirms that some road users are not aware or understand the meaning of some traffic signs.

Driving Mirrors

The Advanced Driver is aware of the situation behind as well as to the front of him, by making proper use of the mirrors. This can only be achieved by self-discipline and practice. There are drivers who look in the mirrors, but do not make effective use of what they see well before signalling, changing direction, slowing down and stopping, thus committing a dangerous act or offence.

The proper use of the mirrors at the right time and place is part of the System of Car Control: if a driver omits to use the mirrors at a given time or place, the System is incomplete and could be dangerous.

'Driver' Signals

Signals are the means by which drivers warn other road users of their intention and presence. There are three types of visible signal fitted to every new car: the direction indicator signals, stop lamps and headlamps; and the driver's arm signal makes a fourth. They are the language of the road, and are the only visible way drivers can inform other road users and pedestrians of their intention and presence.

To be of any use, signals must be given clearly as illustrated in the *Highway Code*, and at the right time and place — ie Feature Two of the System of Car Control. If no other road user or pedestrian is in sight then a signal is superfluous. However, it should be considered again at Feature Four of the System.

Far left:
Another example of a driver who is apparently not aware of the advice given in the *Highway Code*.

Left:
Rumble strips within white lines are being used on the edge of some carriageways, to warn road users of the potential danger of ill-defined verges. Should the rumble strip be driven on, the driver will feel vibration through the steering wheel, therefore a change in course should be made.

Right:
One of the most dangerous roads carrying two-way traffic is the one marked with three lanes. To reduce the possibility of accidents, and to assist the movement of traffic at peak times, a restriction to the use of the centre lane applies after the time shown on the traffic sign.

A signal gives a warning, not an instruction, and gives no right of way whatsoever to carry out an intended action. Too many serious accidents are caused by drivers and motorcyclists who signal their intention to carry out a manoeuvre without taking rear observation before changing course, regardless of the position and speed of other road users who could be following or overtaking them at the time.

Stop Lamps

The stop lamps are fitted to the rear of the vehicle and are illuminated when the foot brake pedal is pressed. They provide a useful signal in circumstances where advance warning should be given of the intention to slow down or stop. It must be borne in mind that the stop lamps will not illuminate until the brakes are applied; it is also of utmost importance that the mirrors are used before applying the footbrake.

Headlamps

The flashing of headlights should not be used for signalling in daylight unless in lieu of a horn warning for overtaking at speed on motorways, dual carriageways and other fast roads: on these the application of the System and, therefore, the warning of approach will be earlier than on other types of road. The length of the warning will be determined by circumstances, but in any case should consist of only one flash.

Arm Signal

The arm signal should be given to emphasise an intention or to confirm a mechanical signal already given, more so in bright sunshine when the direction indicators might not be seen due to the brightness of the sun reflecting on the indicators. An arm signal should be used when slowing down on the approach to a pedestrian crossing: in so doing, pedestrians will be aware of your intention to slow down or stop.

One signal many drivers do not use these days is an acknowledgement of a courtesy extended by another road user. All the driver should do to indicate appreciation is raise a hand; it should not be overdone, but nor should it be neglected, because its general use can do much to promote good road manners.

11 Level Crossings

There have been numerous serious and fatal accidents at level crossings; some due to driver error and some to stupidity on the part of the driver. Some accidents have occurred for which the real cause will never be known. There are different types of level crossings; some have signals that control the movement of traffic over them, and some do not.

Left:
This crossing has half barriers. Amber lights have started to flash and an audible alarm is being given, thereby warning the driver that the barriers are about to be lowered. The mirrors have been used and speed is being reduced by proper use of the brakes. There is no option but to stop at the crossing.

Right:

The information given by the warning sign and 'count down' markers give a clear warning of the potential danger ahead. The mirrors must be used and preparation made to slow down and stop should the lights on the sign ahead start to flash.

Far right:

The sign ahead gives no warning when a train approaches. Therefore the driver must use the mirrors and reduce speed. If the radio is switched on it should be turned off and windows wound down, thereby assisting the driver to listen for an approaching train; effective observation to both sides should be taken to make sure there is no train approaching. If no train is approaching, the driver can proceed over the crossing.

Right:

There is only a warning sign, no barriers or flashing lights. The view of the railway line to the right is totally obscured by a tall hedgerow. The mirrors should be used and speed reduced so that the crossing can be approached at walking speed. If in any doubt 'Stop'.

12 Breakdowns

There is an old proverb that has proved itself to be true on many occasions, this being: 'A dirty vehicle becomes a neglected vehicle, a neglected vehicle becomes a dangerous vehicle'. Thus many breakdowns are the result of neglect, abuse, lack of routine checks and maintenance. However, even a well maintained vehicle can break down.

In the event of a breakdown or puncture the driver should, if possible, get the vehicle off the carriageway. If, for one reason or another this is not possible, the hazard lights should be switched on. The driver and any passenger(s) should then leave the vehicle by the nearside door and get clear of the road. Children must be kept under strict control. Keep animals in the car. The driver should then take appropriate action to warn other road users of the obstruction, by using the hazard warning lights. Should a breakdown occur during the hours of darkness, the obligatory (side) lights should be left on together with the hazard warning lights.

In poor daytime visibility and in heavy rain, mist and fog, the same procedure should be carried out as for the hours of darkness. If a red warning sign is in the vehicle it should be placed 50m (55yd) from the vehicle if the road is straight, and, if you breakdown just after a bend or hump-back bridge place the triangle on the approach to the bend or bridge so that drivers will see the triangle before the broken-down vehicle. Should equipment and or spare wheel have to be removed from the rear of the vehicle to

Below left:
Should your vehicle breakdown just after a bend, place the advance warning triangle before the bend, thereby warning approaching drivers of the hazard ahead.

Below:
If your vehicle breaks down on a motorway or dual carriageway which has a 70mph speed limit, the warning triangle should be placed at least 150m (165yd) from the vehicle. A vehicle breakdown on a motorway can be very expensive, more so if you are not a member of a national association who deal with breakdowns.

Right:
If possible stop near an emergency telephone.

Far right:
Walk on the inside of the hard shoulder.

Below right:
The embankment is the safest place to wait while waiting for assistance to arrive.

assist in the repair of the breakdown, every precaution should be taken by the driver, or any one else, not to obscure the rear lamps and hazard warning lights from approaching traffic, thus defeating their purpose.

Because of the tragic and unpleasant happenings that have occurred to female drivers after their vehicle has broken down, while travelling alone, Driver Services of the Royal Society for the Prevention of Accidents, gives the following advice to female drivers under the heading 'RoSPA Advice for Female Drivers on Motorways — Vehicle Breakdown' which has been agreed by the Department of Transport, Police and motoring organisations:

- 1. If practicable leave at the next exit.
- 2. Otherwise, switch on hazard warning lights and stop on the hard shoulder as far to the left as possible.
- 3. Try to stop near the emergency telephone.
- 4. Leave the vehicle by the nearside door. This includes any passengers. Keep animals in the car. If possible lock all doors except the front passenger door.
- 5. Walk to the nearest telephone keeping to the nearside of the hard shoulder. Arrows on marker posts which are situated at the back of the hard shoulder, will direct you to the nearest emergency telephone. No money is required to use the phone.
- 6. The emergency telephone provides immediate contact with the police. Tell them you have broken down and any specific help you require. If you are a woman on your own ensure this is made clear.
- 7. Return to the vicinity of your vehicle so that you can see help arrive. The embankment is the safest place. There is a greater risk of an accident on the hard shoulder than being attacked. If you feel threatened return immediately to your car, lock all doors until any perceived danger has passed.
- 8. DO NOT attempt repairs on the offside of your vehicle, even changing a wheel. Seek assistance, use the emergency phone.
- 9. DO NOT cross the carriageway in any circumstances.
- 10. DO NOT use the hard shoulder except in an emergency.

13 Stopping and Parking

A driver who intends to park his vehicle should, whenever possible, use a car park. If the vehicle has to be parked on the road, information given by traffic signs or road markings must be complied with, otherwise an offence could be committed for stopping at the wrong time and place. The driver should bring his vehicle to rest in a safe position close to and parallel with the kerb. It cannot be emphasised enough that the *Highway Code* should be complied with whenever a vehicle is parked, except in circumstances beyond the driver's control, or to avoid an accident; otherwise an offence will be committed. If the vehicle has to be parked on an uphill gradient, leave the steering wheel turned to the right; thus if the vehicle should roll back, the front wheels will be stopped by the kerb. The handbrake must be firmly applied and, as an additional safety measure, select first gear. When parking on a downhill gradient, turn the steering wheel to the left, then select reverse gear.

Below left:
Turn the steering wheel to the right when parking on an uphill gradient.

Below:
When you park on a downhill gradient, turn the steering wheel to the left.

Right:
No Stopping restrictions are indicated by signs and road markings. *RED* lines along the road parallel to the kerb mean *NO STOPPING AT ALL*, not even to pick up or drop off passengers.

Below right:
The driver of this car thought it was a convenient place to park; the law thought otherwise, therefore the wheel clamp.

Reverse Parking

Parallel with the kerb

Finding a safe place to park and complying with the law in most towns is an ever-increasing and often frustrating problem. To be able to park between two cars that are parked parallel with the kerb, you will need a gap that is at least one and a half lengths of your own vehicle. As a matter of comparison, candidates on the 'L' driving test are expected to complete this manoeuvre within two vehicle lengths, but only the leading vehicle will be present. To start this manoeuvre you should stop your vehicle about 1m from the parked vehicle and with the front bumpers level. If the vehicle on your left is shorter than yours, stop your vehicle when the rear bumpers are level, this is to compensate for the different length in vehicles. The handbrake should be applied while keeping your foot on the footbrake then reverse gear should be selected, the reversing lights will inform other drivers of your intention.

Left:

Pull up level with the parked car and get ready to reverse, all round observation must be taken. If it is safe to do so release the handbrake and then ease the clutch pedal up just enough to the biting point.

Bottom far left:

Take all round observation again and, if safe to do so, release the handbrake and allow the car to move slowly and turn the steering wheel hard left. When the car is going towards the kerb take the left steering lock off so that the front wheels are straight.

Below left:

When the nearside door mirror is in line with the off-side rear light of the parked car, turn the steering wheel hard right, at the same time looking to make sure your vehicle is clear of the parked vehicle.

Right:
As the front of the vehicle gets near the kerb, turn the steering wheel to the left.

Below right:
The vehicle should now be level and parallel with the kerb.

Bottom far right:
To complete the manoeuvre make sure there is equal distance from your car, the vehicle in front, and the vehicle behind, otherwise when you return to your vehicle you could be boxed in.

Reversing into a Side Road

During a driver's career, the need to turn his vehicle round to face the opposite direction can arise on many occasions. One of the most difficult and potentially dangerous manoeuvres is that of a 'U' turn, usually a safer alternative is to reverse into a side road on the left. This manoeuvre has its potential dangers, more so when pedestrians are present on the foot path. For this reason the driver should select a suitable corner where danger and inconvenience to pedestrians and other road users are at a minimum. A driver who has to reverse a commercial vehicle round a corner should bear in mind the large area to the rear of the vehicle that is blind to him, and should obtain assistance from a reliable person.

Far left:
Pull up just past the corner and get ready to reverse; all round observation must be taken. When you are sure it is safe to reverse, release enough clutch so that the vehicle moves slowly, bearing in mind that what is currently a safe situation could suddenly change.

Above left:
Before turning the steering wheel take all around observation again; if in doubt STOP.

Far left:
When you are sure it is safe to continue, do so. At the same time you must be aware of the potential dangers that could arise.

Left:
There is no need to reverse more than necessary. When you stop carry out the procedure for moving off.

Right:
A suitable position has been found clear of trees and lamp posts near the kerb. The driver is ready to move off, the mirrors have been used and he is looking round to get unobscured observation. When he is sure the road is clear and no pedestrians are about to pass, the handbrake will be released; the vehicle should be moved slowly and smoothly and at the same time the steering wheel should be turned quickly to the right.

Far right:
The driver has applied full right lock and is looking to his offside. When the front offside wheel is about 4ft from the kerb the steering wheel should be turned quickly to the left.

The Turn Round in the Road

The alternative to reversing round a corner is to turn the vehicle round in the road. The majority of qualified drivers today are aware of this manoeuvre, as it was part of their training for the 'L' test. The driver should find a side road that is suitable so that the manoeuvre can be completed as safely as possible. It is possible, particularly with a vehicle fitted with power assisted steering, for sufficient effort to be exerted on the steering wheel to move the road wheels when the vehicle is stationary. This practice should be avoided because of the strain imposed on the steering linkage. Therefore the steering wheel should not be moved unless the vehicle is moving.

One of the reasons why some drivers fail the advanced Driving Test is lack of judgement and control whilst manoeuvring and reversing.

Right:
The steering wheel has been turned to the left, the vehicle has been brought to a stop. The handbrake will be applied because the road has a camber. Reverse gear will be selected and all round observation taken, if clear the handbrake will be released and the steering wheel will be turned to the left. The driver will look over his left shoulder while applying full left lock.

Far right:
When full left lock has been applied, the driver should look over his right shoulder.

Far left:
The vehicle is stopped as it gets near the kerb. The handbrake is applied and first gear selected. The driver will look right, left and right again; when he is sure it is safe to move off, the handbrake will be released and the vehicle moved slowly and smoothly forward, at the same time turning the steering wheel quickly to the right.

Above left:
With a full right lock applied, the vehicle is moving slowly and smoothly forward.

Left:
Just before the vehicle is level with the kerb, the steering is turned quickly to the left. When the vehicle is level with the kerb, the mirrors must be used; if safe to do so, normal driving may be resumed.

Below:
The driver, seeing a suitable parking space, must use the mirrors and if necessary inform other drivers of his intention. The vehicle should be brought to rest as shown. The driver should then get ready to reverse.

Below right:
All round observation must be taken before the manoeuvre is started; if in any doubt, the driver should wait to make sure it is safe to proceed.

Parking in a Car Park

Parking parallel with another car is a manoeuvre that will in all probability have to be accomplished when visiting a supermarket, public and private car parks, where parking spaces are generally marked out. It is important that this manoeuvre is completed with the vehicle in the middle of a marked space, unless circumstances dictate otherwise. When entering a multi-storey, underground or indoor car parks, use dipped headlights, thereby assisting other drivers and pedestrians to see you.

Stopping and Leaving the Vehicle

A driver who intends to park his vehicle on the public highway should implement Feature Two of the System. The mirrors should be used to check the movements and position of following traffic, bearing in mind that it will be necessary to apply the brakes. A signal by direction indicator or arm should be considered to inform other road users and pedestrians of the intention to deviate or slow down. Speed should be reduced gradually, having due regard to traffic that can be following too closely.

The driver should bring his vehicle to rest in a safe position close to the kerb. It cannot be emphasised enough that the driver must comply with the *Highway Code* whenever he parks his vehicle — except in circumstances beyond his control or to avoid an accident — otherwise he will be breaking the law.

When the driver has brought his vehicle to rest, his foot should remain on the brake pedal until the hand brake is applied and neutral selected. If the vehicle is on a gradient, first gear should be selected if the vehicle is facing uphill, and reverse gear selected for that of a down hill gradient, as an additional safety precaution. The engine and all unnecessary auxiliaries should then be switched off, and the seat belt stored neatly. For a vehicle with an automatic gearbox, the gear selector should be moved to the 'P' position.

The driver should make sure it is safe to get out of the vehicle. He should look in his mirrors and over his shoulder for passing traffic, and only when it is safe to do so, should he open the door. Likewise, a passenger should look over his shoulder to make sure it is safe to open the door, otherwise a pedestrian could be injured.

Before leaving the vehicle unattended, the driver should carry out the following checks:

- Remove the ignition key and activate the steering lock.
- Close all windows.
- Put any valuables out of sight, preferably in the boot.
- Lock all doors, the boot and sun roof.

Left:
The driver is applying full left lock, at the same time taking all round observation.

Bottom far left:
The driver has checked the nearside, and is now making sure there is adequate clearance on his side.

Below left:
When the manoeuvre is completed, the vehicle should be parallel with the markings of the parking space, and equi-distant from the vehicles on either side. Should the vehicle not be in the centre of the space, the driver must make sure it is safe to move forward, then reverse back into the space making sure there is equal distance to the vehicles to either side of him. The procedure for stopping and leaving the vehicle should be implemented.

14 Single Track Roads

Speed is the last thing that should be considered when travelling along a single track road. A driver should make due allowance for the possibility that another vehicle may appear around the next bend. It must be understood that the combined speeds of two opposing vehicles will reduce the distance available for stopping, compared with those given in the *Highway Code*. Should one or both of the drivers not be concentrating on their driving, a serious accident could occur. The average driver takes 0.7sec from seeing an emergency to placing his/her foot on the brake pedal.

Above right:
The traffic sign gives clear advice and warning.

Right:
Use a passing place to let oncoming traffic pass or for allowing following vehicles to overtake.

Far right:
Keep your speed down when pedestrians and/or animals are about. Reduce speed on the approach to bends.

15 Audible Signal: The Horn

The horn should be used when it is really necessary. For example, when all other precautions have been taken, it may be of necessity to attract the attention of another road user, pedestrian or cyclists who is unaware of your approach.

The advanced driver's experience and intuition must be the criteria upon which the driver decides whether a horn note is required. In heavy traffic the use of the horn is rare, because speeds are moderate and other actions can be taken in good time. It must be appreciated that the use of the horn gives no protection or right of way whatsoever. There have been fatal accidents caused by drivers using the horn, and in doing so mistakenly assuming the road ahead will be clear by the time the hazard is reached. The horn should be sounded in good time, not in an aggressive manner or in a way that will frighten other road users or pedestrians. The use of the horn must comply with the guidance given in the *Highway Code*.

Above left:
A vehicle can be seen waiting to emerge into the junction. The sun is shining into the driver's eyes, thus causing a distraction. There is also an obstructed view to their right caused by a tree. Therefore the driver waiting to emerge may not be aware of your presence, thus the horn should be used as a warning of your approach.

Left:
A vehicle can be seen reversing from a private drive way. It must not be assumed the driver can or has seen you, therefore the horn should be used.

16 Junctions and Vision

In 1990 there were 155,971 reported accidents at junctions. There were a further 102,470 reported accidents which occurred not at, or within 20m of a, junction. The area ahead and to either side of the driver is divided into zones, what can be seen and what cannot be seen. It is, therefore, essential for a driver approaching a junction, which cannot be seen to be clear, to be sure it is safe to emerge, before the decision to do so can be made.

Below:
Vehicles have been parked too close to the junction, thereby obscuring the view to the left.

Far right:
The driver of the red car parked his vehicle too near the roundabout, thereby forcing passing traffic to approach the roundabout on the wrong side of the road.

Top far left:
Parked vehicles on the roundabout will obscure your view of approaching traffic.

Above left:
The private wall obscures your view of any approaching traffic; therefore speed should have been reduced so that you can stop in the distance that can be seen to be clear.

Left:
When intending to turn right where dead ground is present, the view of the road ahead is restricted. By looking through the hedgerow, a driver will be able to look across the bend and see any approaching traffic.

Right:
If it is not clear to complete the turn, wait where you are until it is safe to do so.

Below right:
Some roundabouts have two or more lanes on the approach, but only one lane on its exit. Common sense must prevail; let the other driver have the right of way.

Bottom far right:
Your view of a road junction should also include the road surface. In this example tyre marks can be seen. When it rains rubber dust mixed with oil will be washed to the road surface, thereby turning the roundabout into a skid pan.

17 Driving Through Water

Driving at speed on surface water and in heavy rain can be hazardous, because water-logged tyres will lead to 'aqua planing', more so when the tread depth of the front tyres is near the legal limit. 'Aqua planing' is a condition when the front tyres cannot cope with undispersed surface water due to the volume of it and the speed of the vehicle, usually in excess of 50mph. When this happens, the tyres push superfluous water forward, creating a wedge; given time and distance, the tyres will mount the wedge and lose contact with the road. The symptoms of 'aqua planing' are light steering and, if speed is maintained, complete loss of steering control will occur. If 'aqua planing' is suspected, deceleration must be immediate, by reducing pressure from the accelerator but not by braking — even momentarily — because this will aggravate the condition. When road speed has been reduced considerably the tyres will regain contact with the road surface, and steering control will be regained.

Driving at speed into unsuspected deep water — eg, puddles or deep ruts — will, in all probability, wrench the steering wheel from the hands of the driver, as the wheel reaches the deepest point of the puddle or rut. In consequence, the driver will lose control.

Flood water will collect quickly due to heavy rain or melting snow, especially in poorly drained low lying areas or uneven road surfaces, at the sides of a cambered road, and where there is a dip under a bridge or underpass.

Many drivers disregard adverse weather conditions and drive too fast for the prevailing conditions. Maintaining an excessive speed in poor visibility caused by spray thrown up by large goods vehicles and/or the density of rain, will make flood water difficult to detect on any type of road; this creates potential danger to the driver and other road users.

Far left:
Driving at speed into deep puddles will, in all probability, wrench the steering wheel from the hands of the driver.

Left:
The driver of the van is obviously not aware that he could have caused a serious accident.

Below:
The decision to overtake has been made. The road ahead can be seen to be clear, and the vehicle about to be overtaken is travelling on a steady course.

Below right:
The decision to overtake has been made. The road ahead can be seen to be clear, but the vehicle that is to be overtaken is drifting to the centre line. In this situation the horn should be considered and the manoeuvre cancelled.

18 Overtaking

Thoughtless overtaking at the wrong time and place has been the cause of many fatal road accidents. During his journey, a driver will pass many stationary and moving vehicles; those travelling in the dame direction as himself he is said to 'overtake'. To do so safely, the System of Car Control must be applied. Although the System is the same as for fixed hazards, it is more complex, because, during the process of overtaking, a number of subsidiary hazards may arise and have to be dealt with in conjunction with the primary hazard.

Passing a stationary vehicle on the nearside of the road requires some thought, but presents little difficulty. The mirrors must be used well before applying Feature One (Course), and moving out to pass the obstruction. The driver must consider using each Feature of the System in sequence and as necessary.

Left:
As stated, thoughtless overtaking has been the cause of many fatal accidents. This driver is trying to overtake two vehicles, with a clear road ahead there should be no difficulty, but vehicles can be seen approaching thus causing a problem. The overtaking driver has no option but to cancel the idea of overtaking the second vehicle.

Below left:
Another example of poor judgement. A driver has started to overtake when an oncoming car can be seen. To continue on his present course of action could prove fatal.

19 Motorways and Dual Carriageways

Highway transportation is a vital factor in the economic and social life of a country. This is particularly so of motorways — truly the arteries of the land — for without them millions of vehicles would grind to a halt, adding chaos to our already overcrowded roads. Today motorways are the arteries of the world's land transport systems carrying commuters and cargo, private and public users.

Motorways have been designed and constructed to provide safer travelling, reduce the time taken to make a journey, and to carry more traffic. This objective has been achieved, making a significant contribution to the national economy and being a benefit to the community.

For a variety of reasons, new Parliamentary powers were needed to construct the new special roads. In 1949 the Royal Assent was given to the Special Roads Act of 1949, which made possible the building of roads such as motorways for the exclusive use of certain types of motor traffic. Those types not included are banned from motorways completely. The Act also gave the necessary powers to alter or close any side road, public footpath or private driveway which crosses the route of the special road.

The first motorway constructed in the United Kingdom was the Preston By-pass officially opened on 5 December 1958 by the Prime Minister, Mr Harold Macmillan. It was eight miles long and is now part of the M6. The next motorway to be constructed was the London-Yorkshire M1. Mr Ernest Marples opened 72 miles of motorway between Aldenham and Crick on 11 April 1960.

When designing a motorway, surveyors and engineers have to include many safety factors. The average driver is not aware of these, which appear to be taken for granted.

Standards of Alignment

On some motorways there are curves but no bends. Due to the higher speed that traffic travels on motorways, compared with other types of road, it is essential that a driver has a good view of the road ahead. It should be understood that 'sight distance' is the clear distance over which a driver, entering a curve, is able to see an obstruction from an assumed eye level of 3ft 6in above the surface of the road. The minimum sight distance required along rural motorways is 295m (950ft), in both vertical and horizontal planes. This sight distance is equivalent to the minimum stopping distance for a speed of 70mph while travelling round a curve, if there was an obstruction ahead. A vehicle travelling at 70mph would cover a distance of 950ft in 9sec.

Considering the preliminary alignment of the route, the design layout of a motorway supplied by the surveyor has to incorporate the significance of sight distance in relation to the curvature, bridges and other fixtures that could obstruct a driver's view, with economics in mind.

It must be borne in mind that smooth and hard wearing road surfaces are provided on motorways, but these may have a very low coefficient of friction when wet. In adverse weather conditions, the stopping distance should be at least trebled.

After travelling some distance on a motorway, there is a tendency for a driver to increase speed without being aware of the fact. Long straight stretches can have a hypnotic and monotonous effect and can affect a driver by what is called Parallelism, especially when the driver is tired. This is why motorways have curves, to prevent Parallelism and help the driver remain alert.

Joining and Leaving a Motorway

Drivers join a motorway from a slip road that progresses into an acceleration lane. The majority of slip lanes have a downhill gradient, thereby assisting the driver to increase his road speed to that of traffic on the motorway. Most acceleration lanes are parallel to the main carriageway and are about 800ft in length.

A driver must give way to traffic on the carriageway. If he forces his way into the traffic on the motorway, he is committing an offence, and in so doing is causing drivers to brake or change course to avoid a collision. If a signal is used when joining a motorway, it gives no right of way whatsoever.

Road Works

However well a motorway has been constructed, there will come a

Above left:
When on the acceleration lane of a motorway, use the mirrors and look over your right shoulder, thereby making sure the presence and position of any traffic on the carriageway is known.

Above:
By making effective use of the mirrors you will be aware of the position of any following traffic. This is essential before a change in course is made.

time when resurfacing or major repairs will be required. As motorways were constructed in lengthy sections, it follows that repairs could extend for several miles with consequent traffic restrictions. This must be borne in mind by the driver who intends to use the motorway while repairs are being carried out.

Road works must be planned carefully, not only to minimise the risk of accidents to the workmen and to users of the motorway, but also to complete the work in the shortest possible time. As a last resort, one side of the carriageway will have to be closed. In such an event, traffic from one side of the motorway will be diverted through the gap in the central reservation (ECP) to the opposite side of the carriageway; this is called 'contra-flow'. Every precaution should be taken when travelling in what has become a two-way traffic system.

Crawler Lanes

On motorways, the normal maximum longitudinal gradient in rural areas is 3% (1 in 33). In hilly country a 4% (1 in 25) gradient may exist, when a 1:33 gradient could not reasonably be achieved because of the high cost of deep excavation and other factors involved.

The relative speed differential between classes of vehicles going up a gradient can vary considerably. To minimise the danger of rear-end collisions between fast and slow moving vehicles, an additional motorway lane is sometimes provided on the nearside, called a 'Crawler Lane'. There are four times as many accidents on 'A' Class roads compared with motorways, but when accidents do occur on motorways, owing to the speed (or the differential in speeds), they are frequently of the high impact type, and this in many instances accounts for drivers and passengers being trapped in their cabs and cars, with a very high risk of fire.

When horrific concertina crashes occur, it is usually due to vehicles bunching in periods of limited visibility: speed is not reduced on the approach to fog, thus entering the fog at a speed far in excess for the conditions prevailing. It cannot be emphasised enough that Feature Two of the System (Mirrors, Signals and Speed) must be applied on the approach to fog and mist. The average driver does not think there is any danger ahead, until it is seen, then it is too late to take evasive action. In consequence, another pile up has occurred.

Service Areas

On some motorways, 24hr service areas with adequate parking for private and commercial users are provided. The services available include fuel, a cafeteria or restaurant and toilet facilities; some service areas have emergency repair facilities and overnight accom-

Right:

You must keep a safe distance from the vehicle in front. A good guide to achieve this is to allow at least 1m gap for each mph of your speed, eg 60mph=60m, on a dry road surface, and doubled when the road surface is wet, eg 50mph=100m. To assist drivers to recognise, and thus achieve, a good separation distance, this sign combined with road markings gives a clear idea. The chevrons are 3m long and 40m apart.

Below right:

Cows are crossing a dual carriageway.

modation. It is the responsibility of every driver to ensure that the vehicle he is driving is in a roadworthy condition and capable of completing the journey. It can be too late when instrument readings and warning lights inform the driver of impending mechanical failure: it can also be very expensive. Before travelling on a motorway, the driver must check the vehicle fluid levels, tyres (including the spare), tools, fan belt, lights and windscreen wipers/washers and ensure that the wheels are secure, that all glass is clean and that all electrical systems are working. In winter, anti-freeze should be added to the cooling system.

The book, titled *Safer Motorway Driving* by Gordon Cole and published by Ian Allan, is designed to give experienced drivers and first-time users an outline of how to drive safely on the fastest and safest roads available to us today.

Dual Carriageway

A dual carriageway is similar in some respects to a motorway, but not in others. The speed limit on some dual carriageways can be the same as that of motorways. However, the legal powers obtained in the Special Roads Act 1949 restrict motorways to the exclusive use of certain motor traffic, thus allowing a certain specific class of traffic to use it. There are no such restrictions on classes of traffic that can use a dual carriageway.

When driving on a dual carriageway, many drivers travel too fast where hazards exist, because they do not recognise actual or potential danger, believing that the other road user will stop, or that they will be able to stop whatever happens. Speed must be governed by the amount of road that can be and cannot be seen to be clear, and the driver must always be able to stop within the range of his vision by day or by night. An average family saloon travelling at 70mph on a dry road surface will on either type of road take approximately 315ft (22 car lengths) to stop; adequate distance from the vehicle in front must therefore be maintained at all times.

Far left:
The speed limit is 70mph and there are cross roads ahead.

Left:
There is dead ground ahead. There is also the possibility of vehicles emerging from a garage.

Bottom far left:
One vehicle is using the slip lane, while other vehicles are crossing the carriageway.

Below left:
When crossing a dual carriageway, bear in mind that approaching traffic travelling at 70mph, will cover a distance of 103ft/sec.

20 Skidding

Below:
The driver has approached a right-hand bend too fast. In so doing the rear of the car has lost adhesion and veered off to the left. The driver must take corrective measures by putting the clutch pedal down, releasing the accelerator and turning the steering wheel quickly to the left. The driver must be prepared for the possibility of a secondary skid.

Skidding is defined as the involuntary movement of the vehicle due to grip of the tyres on the road becoming less than a force or forces acting on the vehicle. In other words a vehicle skids when one or more of the tyres lose normal grip on the road. Any driver who has experienced a skid will remember that he was changing either the speed of direction of the vehicle immediately prior to the skid developing. It will therefore be realised that skids are usually caused by accelerating, braking or changing direction, these manoeuvres being carried out so suddenly or forcibly that forces are created which are more powerful than the grip of the tyres on the road. It therefore follows that the more slippery the road surface, the less powerful are the forces needed to break the grip of the tyres.

The following are causes of skidding, either singly or in combination:

- Excessive speed for the existing circumstances — this is a basic and common cause.
- Course steering in relation to speed which is not in itself excessive.
- Harsh acceleration.
- Harsh or sudden braking.

It is therefore essential that each type of skid is recognised in the early stages of development if corrective measures are to be taken.

Rear Wheel Skid
This occurs when the rear wheels lose their grip on the road and the vehicle may swing to either direction. If unchecked, the rear wheel skid can cause the vehicle to turn broadside or completely round. Eliminate the cause by relaxing pressure on the accelerator or brake pedal, and at the same time turn the steering wheel in the direction of the skid, ie if the rear wheels slide to the left, turn the steering wheel to the left. When stability has been regained the vehicle can be steered on to the desired course. Excess or prolonged steering correction should be avoided or another skid may be induced in the opposite direction.

Front Wheel Skid
This occurs usually on a corner or bend when the front wheels lose their grip, and the vehicle does not travel in the direction in which it is being steered. It can be caused by excessive speed, coarse steering or excessive or sudden braking, and in the case of a front wheel-drive vehicle, harsh acceleration. Eliminate the cause by relaxing the accelerator or brakes, momentarily straighten the steering to allow the front wheels to regain their grip, and then

gently steer on to course. In front wheel drive vehicles the driver should be prepared for the sudden grip of the front wheels as deceleration becomes effective.

Four Wheel Skid

This occurs when all wheels lose their grip on the road. It is usually associated with excessive or sudden braking, and the effects on the vehicle may be a combination of those encountered in a rear or front wheel skid. On slippery surfaces the driver may experience a sensation of an increase rather than a decrease of speed. The next action will normally be dictated by traffic conditions, but usually there is need for a quick reduction in speed. On dry roads this will be achieved by maintaining the pressure on the brake pedal. Where, however, directional control is more important, and in all cases on wet or slippery roads, the cause of the skid must be eliminated by relaxing the pressure on the brake pedal, thus allowing the wheels to revolve again to regain control. It should be remembered that a four wheel skid may also be a progression from a front or rear wheel skid which has not been corrected.

When driving on very slippery roads, smooth control is essential. Any braking, steering or gear changing must be carried out so that tyre adhesion is not broken. When moving off or travelling at low speeds the selection of a higher gear than normal may be advantageous to reduce the possibility of wheel spin.

General

If a skid is allowed to develop fully a driver will rarely find that he has enough space to correct it. Concentration and good observation are essential if skids are to be avoided, and quick reactions are necessary when a skid does occur.

It is important to stress that on very slippery roads, the best control of speed is through the accelerator with a suitable gear engaged. Reduction of the speed on a slippery surface is best done by the selection of a lower gear, but it is essential that the gear change is made as smoothly as possible with accurate matching of engine revolutions to the road speed before the clutch is finally engaged.

Skidding instruction is given for three reasons:

(a) To raise the standard of driving, to give the highest degree of all-round efficiency.

(b) To give confidence in driving under any conditions.

(c) To equip the driver to meet any emergency which might arise.

It must be borne in mind that skidding must *not* be practised on public roads.

Far left:
The driver has approached a left-hand bend too fast. In so doing the rear of the car has lost adhesion and veered off to the right. The driver must take corrective measures by putting the clutch pedal down, releasing the accelerator and turning the steering wheel quickly to the right. The driver must be prepared for the possibility of a secondary skid.

Left:
Inspector Keith Lyndon of the West Midlands Police demonstrating skid control on a Skid Car. Skidding instruction is given for three reasons:

- **(a) To raise the standard of driving to give the highest degree of all-round efficiency;**
- **(b) To give confidence in driving under any conditions;**
- **(c) To equip the driver to meet any emergency which might arise.**

It must be borne in mind that skidding must not be practised on public roads and car parks.

21 Final Thoughts

The Two Second Rule

What is the two second rule? It is a simple method of keeping a safe distance between you and the vehicle in front, at any speed. The importance of separation distances has been explained throughout this book, and they should be remembered at all times. As a basic reminder; on the open road, one yard for every one mile per hour should be maintained — so a car travelling on a dry road at 50mph should have a gap of 50 metres from the vehicle in front. As the speed increases so does the distance from the vehicle in front. As a guide, when driving in built-up areas at a speed below 20mph a minimum distance of one foot for every one mile per hour should be allowed. As the vehicle leaves the built-up area and the road speed increases, so must the distance from the vehicle in front. Horrific accidents have occurred because all the drivers involved thought they could stop in time; they didn't. There are many drivers today who wish they had kept a safe distance from the vehicle in front.

At night, in built-up areas where visibility is poor, dipped headlamps should be used so that the driver's view is extended and other road users can see his vehicle more easily. A distance should be maintained so that the light from the dipped headlamps do not dazzle the driver in front. The headlamps must be correctly set so as to provide maximum illumination of the road without causing other drivers to be dazzled.

One essential fact to be remembered when driving at any time is that the driver should always be able to stop his vehicle well within the distance he can see to be clear. At night the driver's view is restricted more so when it is raining, therefore speed should be reduced and the following distance from the vehicle in front extended.

Passing Thought

Whenever you are driving on the road and you find yourself in a position such that you have to swerve or brake hard to avoid another road user, pause before you blame the other driver. Rather, consider whether you should have been there, and what would have happened if you had been going at twice the speed!